The
Last Race
of the
20th Century

The Last Race of the 20th Century

by

Jude Wanniski

Polyconomics, Inc.
86 Maple Avenue
Morristown, New Jersey 07960

Library of Congress Catalog Card Number: 98-87724

ISBN: 0-938081-13-6

10 9 8 7 6 5 4 3 2 1

Contents

Introduction

Why would anyone want to read a book about one of the least interesting presidential races of this century? From start to finish, the 1996 Clinton-Dole contest appeared to be no race at all, with President Bill Clinton certain to easily win re-election against Bob Dole, the Senate Majority Leader. And so he did. Yes, I think it could have been won by Dole, which is what kept it so interesting to me from start to finish, but that is not what led me to undertake the writing of this book. It is because I came to see this last race of the century as a stepping stone into the next – a contest not so much of political personalities as of spent political forces. It was a campaign that on the surface had almost nothing to say about the future, despite all the President's talk about building bridges to the next century. This, I think, is why fewer than half of all eligible voters cast ballots, even with Ross Perot's independent candidacy providing a third choice.

Yet as the last gasp of an era that began with the end of the power of monarchy in World War I, it does have within it the seeds of the epoch just ahead. The United States is now clearly the Global Sovereign, alone at last atop the power pyramid of the world for the first time in history. The rest of the world, without exception, knows and accepts the fact that the U.S.A. is the boss and probably will be for centuries to come. What kind of boss will we be? The 1996 presidential race only hinted at this kind of discussion, but because of the prime focus on domestic policy and the nature of the partisan combatants, Clinton and Dole, it never ripened to the level of debate. It must and will in the first race of the 21st century. It is the intent of this book to help prepare the reader for what to expect.

Introduction

As a participant at the edges of the campaign, I was able to observe it from different points of view. I'd known Bob Dole since 1969, writing about his freshman term in the Senate when I was the political columnist for the Dow Jones weekly, *The National Observer*. My closest contact with him was as an outside, unpaid, informal advisor to him during the first two years of the Clinton administration from 1993 to 1994; it was within this period I wrote him some 200 memos, statements or speeches, many of which he acted upon. Disappointed in the stance he had chosen as the 1996 race began, I bid him farewell in early 1995 and a few days later I began a successful effort to persuade Steve Forbes to enter the contest for the GOP nomination. I'd also advised Ross Perot in his 1992 campaign, at his invitation early in that year, and in 1996 advised him again.

Working with Perot's man Russ Verney, who ran the Reform Party, I came fairly close to persuading Jack Kemp – since 1976 my closest friend in politics – to accept the Reform Party presidential nomination. When Dole then chose Kemp as his running mate, pulling him out of announced political retirement, I was again a source of steady advice, both through Kemp and through the Dole campaign team. I produced several memos a day through the homestretch of the campaign, trying to find fresh ideas that Dole and his team would find attractive enough to adopt. Kemp advanced each one of the major initiatives I proposed, and each was aborted at one stage or another. My account here is not in any way a chronology, but rather an idiosyncratic perspective designed to offer the reader a better sense of what that race was about. It is not the conventional history having been written in the service of the status quo. I hope it will provide a head start on the dynamics that will define the first race of the new century, which promises to be as fascinating and important as this last was superficially dull. As the last Republican candidate for President whose world view was primarily shaped by World War II, Bob Dole could never break from that powerful influence as the campaign unfolded. President Clinton, a man who avoided military service, was his commander-in-chief. Before the American electorate could get to a new century, it had to have this last fling with the old.

* * * * *

Political journalists who write books about presidential campaigns like to think of themselves as writing "the first cut of history." This is really a modern phenomenon, first undertaken by the late Theodore H. White, who wrote *The Making of a President, 1960,* about the race between John F. Kennedy and Richard M. Nixon. It was the first election in which I cast a vote, choosing Kennedy, although I was not sure he was liberal enough for my tastes at the time. My first great political love, at age 16, was the Democratic nominee of 1952, Illinois Governor Adlai E. Stevenson. I was so sure he would defeat the Republican nominee, Dwight D. Eisenhower, that when he was skunked, I became so sick to my stomach that I had to stay home from school the next day. Because it was so difficult to hate Eisenhower, I'd come to hate Nixon, Ike's running mate in 1952. That was easy to do. I'd come from a family of Pennsylvania coal miners, with my maternal grandfather as far left as one could be in that era without going to jail. I was taught to hate Nixon the way only political adolescents of any age can hate. As a result, the first vote I cast in 1960 was really not for JFK, who I viewed as a competitor of my hero Adlai, but a vote against the despised Nixon. The election had a happy ending for me and so did Teddy White's account of it. My early attraction to politics had led me to a life as a newspaperman, and I was fortunate enough to cover at least a piece of the Kennedy-Nixon campaign – their debate in Los Angeles that fall – during a brief stint at the *Culver City Star-News.*

By 1964, I had moved on to the *Review-Journal* in Las Vegas, Nevada. As the daily political columnist, I'd written about the race that year between President Lyndon Johnson and Senator Barry Goldwater. Once again, I voted for the Democrat not out of any special

Introduction

affection for him, but because I worried that Goldwater would be too quick on the trigger in foreign affairs and too conservative on social policy. I'd had many black friends and roommates while I was an undergraduate at UCLA, and had been impressed with a speech Martin Luther King, Jr., gave at the Las Vegas Convention Center. I had also written a column praising the Black Muslims for being uncompromising in their demands for racial justice. Goldwater's ascetic conservatism seemed cool toward working people in general and Negroes in particular. Still, as a 28-year-old, I'd already shed my early "knee-jerk liberalism," as it was then called. I found myself more attracted to the young Republican politicians in Las Vegas, who were interested in new ideas, than I was with the Democrats, who already had a formula for political success and saw no need to change. By the end of the campaign, I could write that Goldwater had begun a movement that would not end with his overwhelming defeat.

The year also caused me to re-evaluate Richard Nixon, discarding my adolescent hatred of him and for any political figure from then on. This occurred after my editor at the *Review-Journal*, Robert L. Brown, told me he had known and admired Nixon, especially Nixon's grasp of foreign policy and his sense of the emerging importance of the Pacific Rim and Asia. At Brown's suggestion, I read Nixon's biography, *Six Crises*, and felt ashamed that I'd held such an unreasonable hatred for him. Instead of seeing him as a two-dimensional caricature of a "commie witch hunter," I saw in him the Quaker peacemaker who would one day go to China. Two days after election day in 1964, I wrote a column predicting that Nixon would be the GOP nominee in 1968 and that he might pick as his running mate the Nevada Republican, Lieutenant Governor Paul Laxalt, who had just *lost* his run for the U.S. Senate that week. My prediction that Laxalt would win the governorship in 1966 as a stepping stone was fulfilled, and according to the accounts of the 1968 race, Laxalt was among the top five candidates Nixon considered as his running mate before choosing another Catholic GOP governor, Spiro Agnew of Maryland.

It was at this point of my life that I began to have confidence in my ability to make political prophecies. The key was in the lesson I had learned from my editor, Bob Brown, to think through political ideas for myself from every fathomable angle, as I had done in re-evaluating Nixon, instead of always relying upon the ideas of one political faction or party or person. I felt it gave me an edge over other political reporters, or at least those who tended to partisanship. In later years, the experience is what enabled me to see and appreciate the perspectives of several candidates for the same office, as one can appreciate the play on a chessboard, no matter who the contestant, no matter who the winner.

In 1968, although still a registered Democrat, I voted for Nixon, the man I once loathed, instead of the Democrat, Hubert Humphrey, a man I greatly admired. I'd lost confidence in the Democrats' handling of the Vietnam War, having observed its management as a columnist for *The National Observer*, which I had joined in the spring of 1965. In studying the origins of the war, I was especially unnerved by the way the Kennedy administration sanctioned the 1963 military coup in Saigon and murder of our ally, President Ngo Dinh Diem. My youthful liberalism and attraction to the New Deal welfare impulses also had given way to alarm at how profligate LBJ had been in creating Great Society programs. It wasn't entirely unreasonable on his part, I thought at first. The economy was booming in 1965 on the heels of the Kennedy tax cuts that President Johnson enacted in early 1964. Revenues were pouring into the Treasury at rates that persuaded the Democrats they had discovered a bottomless cornucopia of cash. They called their discovery a "New Economics," a variation on Keynesian economics, with which we might fight wars against poverty and communism at home and abroad. By 1968, these fantasies had been dashed by the exponential increases in the costs of the war and the welfare entitlements. These had been compounded by enactment of a war tax in 1967 that overrode the "New Economics." The 10 percent surtax on the income tax weakened the economy and sent revenues even deeper into the red.

Introduction

In his 1968 campaign, Nixon promised a plan to end the war, an end to the Vietnam surtax, and sound Republican management of the poverty programs. I bought the story and so did the electorate.

Through 1971, I remained at the *Observer*, writing about the glacial pace of the exodus from Vietnam and the Nixonian experiments with the economy. I watched the pragmatic Nixon defer his promise to end the Vietnam surtax and in 1969 sharply increase the tax on capital gains, which hardly seemed the Republican thing to do. This gave me my first insight into the difference between the "old money" of corporate capitalism and the "new money" of entrepreneurial capitalism. In February 1971, I met the chief economist of the Budget Bureau in the Nixon administration, Arthur Laffer, who became my first economics teacher during many lunches and telephone lessons. This was also my first contact with what I later came to call "supply-side economics," or the economics of production – quite the opposite of the Keynesian economics of consumption. In August 1971, Nixon took the country off the gold standard for the first time since the Civil War. I was fortunate to have Laffer privately confess to me that he thought it was a monumental error, and explain why it would cause worldwide financial turbulence and undermine the primacy of American banking. He also confided to me that he had learned what he knew from a man he thought the best economist in the world, a Canadian named Robert Mundell. In January of 1972, I transferred within Dow Jones from the *Observer* to the editorial page of *The Wall Street Journal*, at exactly the time Mundell was alone in the world in forecasting a great inflation.

There was no difficulty in deciding between Nixon and Senator George McGovern in the 1972 race. Nixon was inching us out of Vietnam as best he could. Wage and price controls were still in effect from the 1971 decision to go off gold, so the inflation Mundell had predicted was still not a palpable fact. And I still did not know what Laffer's economics was all about. When the inflation hit, the universal view was that it was caused by the Arab oil countries, which had quadrupled the oil price in 1973. At the *Journal*, we had been persuaded by Mundell and Laffer that going off gold caused the oil price to rise, and then everything else. In fact, the gold price had quadrupled before oil did. It was in the years leading up to the 1976 presidential race between President Gerald R. Ford and Jimmy Carter, the former governor of Georgia, that I finally got my arms around the economics. It also dawned on me, to my horror, that the demand-side economics of consumption, which was at the heart of public finance in both political parties, could only lead to national economic collapse. In the Spring 1974 issue of *The Public Interest*, I wrote *The Mundell-Laffer Hypothesis: A New View of the World Economy*. In the fall of 1974, I interviewed Mundell for the *Journal* editorial page in an article titled, "It's Time to Cut Taxes." The first elected politician I tried to sell the idea to was Bob Dole, but I soon realized he did not have the time or inclination to learn a new view of the world. I tried several other Senators with the same result until finally finding my man in Kemp, who had read the interview with Mundell and decided to champion tax cutting, practically out of desperation. His blue-collar district in Buffalo had the nation's highest unemployment rate at 20 percent.

The longer essay got the attention of a 30-year-old political junkie named Jeffrey Bell, who was Ronald Reagan's research director, and Bell attempted to incorporate some of the ideas into the Reagan campaign for the GOP nomination in 1976, but the efforts were botched. In the general election, President Ford's team was not interested in my tax-cut ideas. I made a trip to Atlanta, trying to interest the Carter people in supply-side ideas, but they also were going in the other direction. On election day, my wife and I decided to split our votes, she for Carter, I for Ford. After Carter's election, Jeff Bell decided to run for a U.S. Senate seat on the ideas I had outlined in *The Public Interest*. He also persuaded me to write a book about my general theories, which became *The Way the World Works*, published in the spring of 1978. Bell won the GOP nomination in

Introduction

June 1978 on his tax-cut ideas, unseating five-term Senator Clifford Case. In the general election, though, Bell shifted gears and ran as a cultural conservative, stressing his support for constitutional amendments to ban abortion and permit school prayer. He was defeated by a former professional basketball star, Bill Bradley, who also said he favored tax cuts, but opposed Bell's cultural conservatism. In the midst of the campaign, I resigned from *The Wall Street Journal* and became an entrepreneur, founding Polyconomics, Inc., in Morristown, New Jersey, which gave me the latitude I needed to be an active player in presidential politics.

The supply-side economic ideas of the Bell campaign survived as Reagan began his run for the GOP presidential nomination in 1980. His campaign manager, John Sears, a former campaign aide to Nixon, had been impressed with Bell's astonishing victory over Senator Case. Sears persuaded Reagan to build his campaign around our economic ideas and to bring Jack Kemp into a formal campaign role. Kemp had worked as a summer intern for Reagan in 1967, between football seasons, and Reagan had actually studied economics in college, from 1929 to 1932, when the kind of supply theory Mundell and Laffer were espousing was still being taught. It was a perfect fit all around. It was because of Sears's decision that Reagan pitched his campaign toward economic growth instead of balance-the-budget "fiscal responsibility," and it was the promise of growth that got him to the White House, unseating Jimmy Carter. A third-party candidate, a former Republican congressman from Illinois, John Anderson, collected a small percentage of the popular vote. And for the first time since 1952, the Senate went Republican.

The Reagan landslide of 1984 over Walter Mondale, a former Minnesota Senator who had been Carter's vice president, was instructive in that Mondale boldly campaigned against the Reagan tax cuts. Indeed, Mondale might have lost the nomination to an insurgent, Colorado Senator Gary Hart, who was cautiously opposing Mondale on the tax issue and seemed to have the momentum, until he weakened on the issue a few days before the Illinois primary and was beaten back. A sex scandal then finished him off before he could recover. Reagan campaigned on his "Morning in America" theme, which spent a fortune on unnecessary television advertising, financed by the taxpayers. The stock market was booming and so was the economy, and Reagan was pledging to further reform the tax system in his second term to get the tax rates even lower than he had in his first. The Senate stayed Republican and the House Democratic.

In 1986, there was a bipartisan deal struck on tax reform, one that supply-siders were not exactly happy with. On the plus side, the top marginal income-tax rate was brought down to 28 percent from 48 percent and ordinary income associated with wages, interest and dividends was indexed to protect against inflation. To "pay" for this reform, the capital gains tax was raised to 28 percent from 20 percent and capgains were not indexed to protect against inflation. Real-estate depreciation rules were also tightened, which led to serious declines in real-property values. This further undermined the savings-and-loan industry, which had been savaged by Nixon's 1971 decision to go off gold. Banks can withstand monetary inflations, but S&Ls, which borrow short and lend long, cannot. Immediately after the 1986 tax act, the voters turned the Senate back to the Democrats. Supply-siders crossed their fingers and hoped that the problems associated with these negative aspects of the reform could be corrected after the 1988 elections. We banked on Jack Kemp winning the GOP nomination. Instead, the Republican primaries turned on foreign policy, with Vice President George Bush the only one of the six principal GOP contenders supporting President Reagan in his peace initiatives with Soviet leader Mikhail Gorbachev. I was among the very few advisers who warned Kemp that he could not win the nomination by opposing the President on this critical issue.

When Kemp dropped out of the race as soon as it was clear Bush had it won, the Bush director of research, Jim Pinkerton, called and

Introduction

asked if I could come to Washington to discuss the campaign's economic plank with George W. Bush, the vice president's son, and Michael Boskin, the Stanford economics professor who was to become chairman of President Bush's Council of Economic Advisers. I did so and advised that we were most concerned with the capital gains tax and hoped it could be brought down to 15 percent and indexed against inflation. Bush said his father had no problem with this, and in fact had come to understand its importance when he was in the risky side of the oil business. In the campaign that followed against the Democratic nominee, Massachusetts Governor Michael Dukakis, Bush campaigned vigorously for the 15 percent, indexed rate – along with his pledge not to raise taxes in other areas. The result was another Republican landslide, although the voters still gave the Democrats control of Congress. Bush, after all, had been identified with the austerity wing of the GOP, the balance-the-budget-at-any-cost wing that traced its lineage to Herbert Hoover.

In the four years that followed, President Bush wrapped up the Cold War, with a successful Persian Gulf War thrown in for good measure. But he not only broke his read-my-lips pledge on taxes at his earliest opportunity, his economic team, led by Treasury Secretary Nick Brady and Budget Director Dick Darman, also threw in the towel on the promise to cut the capital gains tax to 15 percent and index gains to protect them against inflation. By November 12, 1991, I'd given up on President Bush's re-election chances. Writing in *The New York Times*, I said: "Unless a serious growth-oriented Republican challenges Mr. Bush, supply-side Reaganauts have no choice but to look for a Democrat in the tradition of John F. Kennedy, the last Democratic leader who put grass roots growth ahead of Fat Cat America's budget-balancing mania."[1]

A week later, Pat Buchanan entered the race for the GOP nomination, denouncing the President for having broken his no-tax

---

1 Jude Wanniski, "Blame Bush for the Recession," *The New York Times*, November 12, 1991, p. A25.

pledge. A few weeks later, a mutual friend connected me and former California Governor Jerry Brown, who threw his hat into the Democratic ring and ran as an offbeat, supply-side tax reformer. As outsiders, neither Buchanan nor Brown got very far, but Brown did throw a scare into the Establishment by winning the Connecticut primary on his call for a "flat tax." He was, though, not sufficiently prepared to defend the idea and his campaign collapsed in the New York primary when New York Senator Pat Moynihan warned that the Brown flat tax would destroy Social Security. In April of 1992, Arkansas Governor Bill Clinton was solidly backed by the Democratic Establishment and the GOP was split down the middle, with President Bush backed by the GOP Establishment, but damaged goods with ordinary people. It was clear a Clinton-Bush contest would rock no boats. Into this political vacuum vaulted Texas billionaire H. Ross Perot, who would run as an Independent.

A few weeks after the famous "Larry King Live" program propelled him into the race, Perot called me on the advice of a friend, Ted Forstmann, the New York financier. A week later I stopped in Dallas and spent several hours talking politics and economics with him. I explicitly told him that his idea of scrapping the entire tax system and writing a new one on a fresh sheet of paper was one the voters could appreciate, but that the Establishment would do anything it could to stop him. "First they will try character assassination," I told him. "Then maybe real bullets." The former was all that was required, given Perot's inexperience as a candidate and the ineptitude of the man chosen by friends to be his campaign manager, Ed Rollins. Rollins had technically been Reagan's campaign manager in 1984 when his bungling, revealed several times in later campaigns, was concealed by Reagan's popularity and Mondale's promise to raise taxes.

After Clinton's easy victory, I found myself without a political lever at or even near the center of power. With neither an elective nor appointive post, Kemp had little choice but to spend the next

Introduction

year or two on the speaking circuit. My working assumption was that he had been beaten so soundly in 1988 and been left with such enormous debts that he would pretend to be running for President in 1996, but would eventually bow out, which is of course what happened. Beginning in early 1985, though, I had developed a close relationship with Federal Reserve Governor Wayne Angell, once I realized he understood the problems Laffer warned me in 1971 would occur by going off the gold standard. Angell and I had traveled to Moscow together in 1989 to advise the state Gosbank and to Beijing in 1993 to advise the People's Bank of China on conversion to a market capitalism. Angell, a Kansan, had gotten his appointment at the Fed via Bob Dole's influence at the Reagan White House. Angell, of course, was eager to see his patron win the GOP nomination in 1996 and urged me to help Dole in the interim. In the spring of 1993, Dole, Angell and I had a Sunday brunch at the Four Seasons in Washington, and we cemented an arrangement by which I would counsel Dole, who as leader of the Republican Party was now the second most powerful political leader in the world.

My relationship with Dole during the next two years was extremely interesting and intellectually satisfying. We spoke only on my visits to Washington, when I would sit for 20 minutes or a half hour in his Capitol office and discuss whatever was topical. Otherwise I communicated through his press secretary, Clarkson Hine, whose office adjoined Dole's and who was responsible for assembling Dole's reading file. Each morning at 5:30 or 6, I would read *The New York Times* and *Wall Street Journal* and write a brief memo that I would fax to Dole via Clarkson. As a guest at my client conference in Boca Raton, Florida, in February 1994, Dole joked that he had two piles of faxes on his desk from me, one four feet high labeled "bad ideas," and one six inches high labeled "good ideas." At our Four Seasons brunch, I had told Dole that he could expect a great many ideas from me, but I would not be offended if he discarded most of them, as long as I knew I was being useful.

At an early meeting in his office, I told Dole I did not think Kemp would run in 1996, that his confidence had been shaken in his 1988 defeat. In any case, I told Dole I would not abandon him in favor of Kemp if Jack chose to run, but would hope that the result would be a Dole-Kemp ticket. The way I put it was this: Jack was a football hero, a champion who was used to the adulation of crowds. He could be defeated one Sunday but come back the next and win. *His defeat in 1988 was the psychological equivalent of losing 100-0 in a Super Bowl.* It will take a long time for him to recover, and he might need a season as a back-up quarterback to be fully repaired. You, on the other hand, were a war hero, used to dodging bullets in a foxhole, with no adulation from the crowds. At the time, I was told by David Gergen, an old friend from the Nixon days who had agreed to go to work at the Clinton White House the same weekend I brunched with Dole, that it was the assumption that Dole would decide not to run and that Jack would.

My most important contribution to Dole was in persuading him to make serious use of a freshman Republican in the Senate, Robert Bennett of Utah, in beating back the Hillary Clinton plan to socialize medicine. Early in 1993, Dole had co-sponsored a smaller version of the Clinton plan proposed by Senator John Chafee of Rhode Island, a GOP liberal, scorned by conservatives as "Clinton Lite." I advised Dole that he could forget the nomination if he presided over enactment of such a plan and that Bennett of Utah, who had become an enormously successful entrepreneur after he turned 40, would be able to guide him to a solution that would not crush small businesses. Dole did so and Bennett developed the strategy that blocked the First Lady's national health scheme. At my urging, Dole also asked Bennett to be his point man in dealing with Treasury's request for bailout money following Mexico's surprise devaluation of the peso on December 28, 1994. With Dole's help, Bennett, Angell and I thought we could push Treasury into helping Mexico roll back the devaluation in exchange for the support of Congress which the

Introduction

Republicans had won control of in the previous month. Kemp, who had decided not to run at this point, joined in the effort to save Mexico's economy. Dole did his best and so did Bennett, whom Dole called his "Mister Mexico," but in the end Dole's inability to grasp the intricacies of what was at stake caused him to throw in the towel. Treasury got its congressional support and Mexico kept its devalued peso and the recession that would follow.

My frustration with Mexico was one of the ingredients that eroded my confidence in Dole. There would be other straws before my break with Dole, although there was never any personal conflict with him. Indeed, the longer I saw Dole close up, the more I realized what a nice fellow he was behind his dark visage and acerbic wit. Reserved and aloof, yes, but even more kind, considerate and generous. In one of my last meetings with him, I told him how I never knew whether or not I liked him, but up close saw how considerate he was to people who many politicians I've known would treat as being inconsequential, a waste of time. Jack Germond, the hard-boiled political writer for *The Baltimore Sun*, observed on a Sunday talk show during the campaign that in a secret ballot in the Senate, Dole would beat Clinton 3-to-1. Above all, in the Congress, Dole was a man of his word.

Dole, though, had a totally different mind set when it came to running for national office. He had been on the losing Ford ticket in 1976 and had been a protégé of Richard Nixon, who had counseled that as a Republican, *You run to the right in seeking the nomination, and run to the left in seeking the presidency.* This, in fact, was one of the reasons Kemp, who had also been counseled by Nixon on national politics, decided *not* to run. Kemp found it most uncomfortable *positioning* himself on matters of ideology or principle. He could fudge to the right, but he could not run to the right. As soon as Kemp decided not to run in 1996, Dole no longer had to worry about his left flank. He could join the pack of conservatives in the

GOP primaries and position himself close enough to the moderate center to win the nomination, which he probably believed he had wrapped up as soon as Kemp was gone. The last conversation I had with Dole was on Monday, January 30, to inform him by telephone from my office that Jack would announce later in the day he would not be a candidate.

From that point on, through the next several weeks, my morning memos to Dole continued, but he was clearly shifting gears in accordance with Nixon's prescription of *running to the right* in seeking the nomination. On a "Meet the Press" appearance, he indicated he might have to rethink his support for affirmative action for African-Americans in light of the report that 62 percent of white males had voted Republican in the 1994 congressional races. A memo of protest from me made no impression, as the following week he told CNN that his first act as President might be to end affirmative action, after he was informed Senator Phil Gramm of Texas, who was also running right, had made that vow. Economic growth or tax cuts suddenly disappeared from his public comments and he began emphasizing the need for a Constitutional amendment to balance the budget, which was a relic from Ronald Reagan's California days but an idea anathema to most supply-siders. Newt Gingrich had put it in his Contract With America and Dole believed he had to pay obeisance to it in order to win the support of Perot fans. Finally, on March 5, the Sunday *New York Times Magazine* appeared with a cover story on Dole written by a young reporter, Ruth Shalit, who wanted "vision" they should remember "Reaganomics" which produced "all these deficits."

No political event had made me so physically queasy since I went to sleep in 1952 knowing Eisenhower had defeated Stevenson. I called Ruth Shalit to make sure the statement was accurate, and she read it back to me from her notes. I then called Clarkson Hine to tell him about how serious this quote was, that *it was a torpedo Dole had*

Introduction

fired which would turn back on him and hit amidships. When I did not hear back from him or Dole, I wrote the following memo to the Senator, dated March 6, 1995:

> Your quote on Reaganomics was an unfortunate setback to your presidential candidacy. On top of your handling of the BBA [balanced budget amendment], it took all the heart out of me, not to mention the Reaganauts who read it and talked to me about it. The mere idea that you still have in your head the idea that Reaganomics ran up the deficit was a chilling reminder that you never bother to ask about these things. (My mother-in-law called my wife after reading the article to tell her about your "awful crack about Reaganomics.") I've told both Bob Bennett and Jack Kemp that I've lost all enthusiasm for your candidacy these past weeks, since Jack dropped out and you moved steadily away from our world view. Kemp says I should not throw in the towel and so does Bennett. As politicians, they may be better able to assess your perspective, but they have no satisfactory explanation for your steady move away from Reagan. I began to write a bridge-burning essay today, but Jack talked me out of it, although I have no idea what I'm supposed to wait for. My recent efforts to pull you back from the path that has failed you every time you have tried it have done no good. The Times article makes it clear I have been of no use to you at all in analyzing the world around you. All Nov. 8 means is that the people want change, but you will eat the hat of anyone who can tell you what the change is about. From a dozen people I've gotten the question, why does Dole want to be President? You didn't answer the question in New Hampshire and you didn't answer it in the Times article. The picture you leave is a man at his desk in the Oval Office, waiting for a problem to appear in his "in basket."

Bob, I still think you are a national asset. You are still the front runner and may somehow find your way to the nomination and the presidency. I think the last two years would have been disastrous without your legislative leadership. I continue to wish you well and if the field does not change, I will probably wind up voting for you in the New Jersey primary. Indeed, I may be of more use to you at a distance than in your corner. At least, you may come to value my opinion more than you have. At the moment, though, I cannot honestly say I can be in your corner, or, indeed, that you want me there.

In the next few days, I half expected to hear from Dole, asking me to reconsider, to explain that he was just kidding about Reaganomics and did not expect the wisecrack to appear in print. When no call came, I had to assume he no longer believed he had to worry about Kemp and the supply-siders and would be just as happy to see me take a hike. *My God,* I thought, *Dole could never beat Clinton if he did not run as a convert to Reaganomics, but chose to run as a deficit hawk. He and Clinton would slug it out over dead issues instead of fundamental issues of global peace and prosperity. The nation and the world are looking to the United States for direction on a new world order in security, diplomacy and the international economy. If this is where Dole would go, we would waste 1996 in meaningless jockeying for power, with nobody getting a serious mandate for change.* After a few sleepless nights, I called Steve Forbes and suggested he run for President. The rest is the historical perspective you will find as you step into this book. I can only promise that it is accurate to the best of my knowledge, and far more interesting than the campaign that was reported. It will definitely give you a running start on the first race of the 21st century.

CHAPTER ONE

Modern Survival Politics

S urvival is the highest priority of any living thing. It is also the highest priority of any institution, including a political party. After the 1994 congressional elections, which turned control of Congress over to the GOP for the first time in 40 years, the Democratic Party became transfixed with the question of survival. Democratic congressional leaders were stunned by the scope of the Republican victories in the House and Senate and the likelihood that the gains would be extended in 1996. The *de facto* party leader, President Bill Clinton, was demoralized by the clear statement made by the voters in rejecting the course he had set for the nation in the first two years of his presidency – and polls showing his approval ratings so low that a second term seemed highly unlikely.

In early 1996, only one year later, the tables had been turned. By making an insightful assessment of what had gone wrong, President Clinton designed a strategic retreat from the path down which he had been taking his party. The President drew upon the advice of a savvy, bipartisan political consultant, Dick Morris, who made it his business to understand the way conservative Americans looked at the political world. At the same time, the GOP, under the new leadership of House Speaker Newt Gingrich, made a series of enormous political blunders. Suddenly, it was the Republican Party that was most concerned about surviving the November 1996 elections. Not only did the President seem an overwhelming favorite for re-election, but the voters also appeared to be in a mood to punish the GOP by giving Congress back to the Democrats. It was in this anxious climate that the Republican organization threw its full weight behind the candidacy of Bob Dole – though not with any confidence that he could win in November, but that he would lose in such a way that would permit the GOP to hold one or both houses of Congress.

There is no place where you can find it written in the archives of the Republican Establishment that it was already conceding the White House to the Democrats before the race even began. You had to *feel* it, the way you sense a football team has given up on the game or the season. On March 1, 1996, it was still not obvious that Dole would be the nominee. The insurgent candidacies of Steve Forbes and Pat Buchanan were still very much alive. If Dole did not do well in South Carolina, into which he had poured serious resources and where he had the solid support of the GOP organization, he would be on the ropes. "At the moment, the Party's organization remains in a defense mode. Its candidate, Bob Dole, is not likely to win the White House, but he would run a safe race, and the GOP would retain control of the Senate and House and not lose much at the state and local level."[1] At that point, the only hope for a Dole victory among GOP leaders rested on the slim possibility that General Colin Powell would change his mind and join the ticket – or that the various scandals surrounding the White House would produce a smoking gun. In any event, the Forbes and Buchanan campaigns essentially collapsed the following day when Dole won by a landslide in South Carolina, a sure sign the GOP organization was not going to take any more chances on an unconventional candidate. It probably could not win with Dole, the GOP seemed to sense, but it wouldn't lose big time as it might with a loose cannon or an unknown quantity.

The second priority of any institution is to expand its reach, to add to its strength. As a candidate, Dole proved successful enough as the organization's man in conducting the kind of campaign that enabled the GOP to maintain not only its political strength, but also its momentum as the party of change. There at least were none of the blunders that might have caused a Democratic sweep and the

---

1 Jude Wanniski, "The Racing Form: Backstretch Primaries," Polyconomics, Inc., Morristown, N.J., March 1, 1996.

Clinton vote was held below 50 percent. We can sum up Dole's failure to win the White House with what seems a simple truism: *He was unable to persuade the country that it could trust the Republican Party with the two elective branches of the national government.* This is a problem the Republicans have faced since the 1928 election of Herbert Hoover. With the single exception of the 1952 election of Dwight Eisenhower, who carried in a GOP Congress on his coattails, the American people have preferred either divided government – with a Republican President being checked by a Democratic Congress, a unified Democratic government, or since 1994, a Democratic President providing a check on a Republican Congress.

Why a check on the Republican Congress? After being out of power for four decades, the House Republicans in the 104th Congress demonstrated a rashness in the pursuit of a limited national government that the electorate had not anticipated and clearly did not want. It obviously prefers the *direction* in which these young Republicans wish to take the country, but not the breakneck pace and not in the sequence of steps chosen by its leader, Speaker Gingrich. It was as if the young Turks had been so impatient with the logjam they had seen forming on the river when the Democrats were in control that they immediately reached for the dynamite. The voters, though, expected a gentler approach, with the key log first being removed and the logjam broken up without blasting.

The Republican Establishment is slowly figuring this out. Perhaps as soon as the national elections in 2000, the voters will decide it can risk giving the GOP its second chance in 70 years to run the show at both ends of Pennsylvania Avenue. The last race of the 20th century was really no accident, although one is tempted to think that all general elections are happenstance. Can't it be that the House of Representatives might swing from one party to the other simply because the voters in 435 congressional districts made up their minds for separate and distinct reasons – having little or nothing to do with the political parties? After every election, we are told that if only one person, or two, in every precinct had voted for the other candidate, the election would have turned out differently. The 1960 presidential race could have gone to Richard Nixon instead of John F. Kennedy if only 12,000 people in three states had voted for him instead of JFK. When Democrats lose, they often complain they could have won if the rich voters were not allowed to give so much money to Republican candidates. When Republicans lose, they often complain that their Democratic opponents used scare tactics to frighten voters into thinking the GOP candidate will vote to take away their Social Security or some other federal benefit.

It is more likely, though, that the voters do the best they can in judging the circumstances and the available candidates they confront at election time. They then have a conversation with each other before deciding on the precise combination of people they will send to Washington. This may be a fanciful way of thinking about the political marketplace, but it is not a bad way of explaining why national elections turn out the way they do and why democracy works as well as it does. There is no other way of explaining how a candidate like Ross Perot in 1992 would shoot to the top of the charts in the presidential preference polls without spending any money. The voters simply had a conversation with each other and put him up there, and then pulled him down. In 1978 in California, an ordinary citizen named Howard Jarvis spent almost no money in persuading the citizens to vote for his proposition that state taxes be cut by a third. The entire political Establishment, Republican and Democratic, spent a fortune trying to persuade the voters that it would be a mistake to do so. The citizens had a conversation with themselves and decided by a 2-to-1 margin that Jarvis was right. When the political establishment is wrong about the direction the country should take, the electorate punishes it in any way that it can. When voting doesn't work, the electorate tries non-voting. If that does not work, parts of the system break down into extralegal forms of political communication, at times violent. It is in this realm we find vigilantes, political assassins, and terrorists.

The process by which the electorate makes up its mind in a national election like that of 1996 is one that must be understood if the Republican Establishment is ever going to be favored by the electorate with a unified government. In the same way, the Democratic Establishment has to do a better job of figuring out why it lost the electorate's confidence in its management of the national legislature and has been relegated to a defensive role in the executive branch. The sorry fact that more than $1 billion was spent on the 1996 elections – much of it raised in scandalous fashion – is palpable evidence that the political Establishment does not understand the efficiency of the political marketplace. It at least acts as if it does not understand that the national electorate is a single organism – a computer that integrates the brainpower of all those eligible to vote. It seems to have dawned on President Clinton sometime after the election that it was not as necessary as he was led to believe that he raise and spend tons of money to persuade the electorate that Newt Gingrich could not be trusted along with a Republican in the White House. For his part, even a year after the election, Gingrich could not be persuaded that his low standing in public esteem was not caused by all the money Democrats and organized labor spent on TV spots that portrayed him in a negative light – even though he seems as unpopular in areas where the spots were not aired as in areas that were saturated with them.

Could Dole have defeated Clinton and brought the Republican Congress back with him? The wisdom of the ages tells us we should not argue with history. Even if we hypothesize that Dole could have done some things differently and edged out Clinton, as we review the history of the options and choices he had, there is no way of assuming the congressional elections would have turned out the way they did. Voters who had not planned to vote might have come in for Dole-Kemp, but cast votes for Democratic congressional candidates at the same time. The electorate thus might have swung enough votes to give the Democrats control of the House, which surely would have meant the instant departure of Gingrich as Republican leader in the House. No, as we will see, there were simply too many chances missed when the Republicans as an institution, might have been able to persuade the electorate that Dole and Gingrich could be trusted at either end of Pennsylvania Avenue. Some of these are chances missed because of Dole's failure to make the right choice when it was in his power to move in one direction or another, although he made some excellent decisions along the way. Most of the errors are simply the result of the Republican Establishment's maneuvering to retain control of Congress, even if this meant losing the White House once again.

All growth, including political growth, is the result of risk-taking. Because of the dynamics of society and the flux of humankind, a government that stands pat ultimately drifts backward. By its very nature, the Establishment of either political party or of the nation itself is risk-averse. As a boy, I remember being charmed by the 1952 Democratic presidential nominee, Adlai Stevenson, when he said "the Republican Party would have to be dragged kicking and screaming into the 20th century." Still, the national electorate preferred Eisenhower and a Republican Congress in 1952 to the risks of an egghead liberal intellectual from Illinois during the trials of the Korean War. Both parties almost always choose *directional* political leaders as their presidential candidates, not legislative leaders who almost always represent consensus. In 1996, the GOP stuck with a consensus candidate and the Democrats gave a second nomination to a new Democrat, who had demonstrated an agility to change direction in the middle of his first term. Clinton had done so with the help of an outside adviser, Dick Morris, who had helped him in similar circumstances in his Arkansas days.

* * * * *

Knowing what we know now, it should be clear even to Senator Dole, who appears willing to shoulder the blame for the outcome, that his main error lay in choosing a campaign manager who lacked experience and competence in this kind of enterprise. Dole's choice of Scott Reed to be his field commander – a young man with no experience in national politics – proved to be a fatal error. Dole did not realize his mistake until it was too late, although it is reasonable to wonder why Dole could ever imagine he could bank on a neophyte as manager. It always seemed a dubious idea, except to those who assumed it meant Dole intended to be his own campaign manager, and Reed would merely be his agent. Reed might have been able to maintain Dole's base of support, but his inexperience almost surely meant he could not expand it to include the constituencies the Senator needed to win the White House. Yet, when Reed seemed to come through for him in the unexpectedly difficult battles of the Republican primaries, the decision looked a little better. At least the political press corps credited Reed with having planned ahead to the March 2 South Carolina primary that turned the tide, Dole winning with sheer organizational muscle.

To be sure, it is easier to understand Dole's choice of Reed if we recall that the decision was made in early 1995, when the political universe assumed that Dole would claim the GOP nomination as a matter of inheritance and trample Bill Clinton on the way to the White House. In 1993 and 1994, Dole as Senate Minority Leader had been for the first time in his 33-year congressional career the undisputed leader of the Republican Party.[2] In 1995, Newt Gingrich would claim the party leadership as the first GOP Speaker in 40 years, but Dole clearly had come off his most successful two years in Congress. He had steered the GOP through the minefields of Clinton's first two years as Democratic President with a Democratic Congress. He had kept the Senate Republicans totally united against the Clinton budget and tax increase. And he had finessed Hillary Clinton's determined attempt to nationalize health insurance.

2 Jude Wanniski, "The Power Pyramid," Polyconomics, Inc., Morristown, N.J., May 12, 1993.

Syndicated columnist Robert Novak had observed Dole throughout his congressional career. As 1994 ended, he wrote that the two years just ended were the best Dole had ever had.

With Dole's favorable ratings in the polls higher than they had ever been, above 60 percent, and Clinton reeling from the loss of Congress for the first time in 40 years, all Dole seemed to need was a bright young man who could keep to a schedule and hire the best political operatives money could buy. Reed had no particular *strategy* for winning the primaries and later never developed a strategy for winning the general election. In the primaries, it probably never occurred to Dole that he would need a strategy. He was the front-runner, and as long as he made no mistakes, he naturally would win. It was taken as a given that Dole far and away was the class of the field, and that he quickly would establish his dominance in the Iowa caucuses and the New Hampshire primary. When Dole barely eked out a victory in Iowa and then lost to Buchanan in New Hampshire, followed by losses to Forbes in Delaware and Arizona, there appeared a brief flurry of rumors about Reed's imminent departure. When Dole then crushed all opposition in South Carolina on March 2, in Dole's eyes his choice of Reed, and Reed himself, was vindicated. There was no need to turn to anyone else.

Still, history will probably conclude that a man who would be President should know that a campaign manager he had chosen when he was at his highest point of public favor and President Clinton at his lowest, would not be appropriate for a campaign in which these positions were reversed. As the campaign ran its course, Reed retreated into his own survival mode, drawing up lists of things to do hour by hour. The only time I spoke directly to Reed in the entire campaign was during the Republican convention in the elevator of the San Diego hotel where Dole had his headquarters. It was early in the morning of the day Dole was to be nominated. We had both stepped into an otherwise empty elevator from the different floors where we were staying. He told me he liked a memo I had sent him about how to go directly at the black vote with ads in black media, which is something that was talked about several times in the months that followed, but which never happened. I came away from that brief conversation with Reed thinking he might already be banking on Clinton's weaknesses and the White House scandals to pull his own man through. There was no reason to expect strategic thinking from the young man, who had gotten the job from Dole when the circumstances were different and a play-it-safe scenario was obviously the correct one to deploy against an unpopular incumbent. To the end of the campaign, Reed did his best not to make any mistakes, when the only way to have won was to risk making them.

With a campaign manager without a strategy,[3] Dole himself moved hour by hour, following instructions and the schedule mapped out for him with little rhyme or reason by a committee of advisors – not one with primary responsibility or accountability. President Clinton never really had to do anything more than ensure everyone knew in his second term that a Republican Congress would not tear down the social safety net that Democrats had been stitching together since 1933. For Dole to win, he had to find a way to persuade the voters that he would do a better job of checking the excesses of a headstrong GOP Congress while mapping out a direction in which the nation could comfortably travel.

Conservative Republicans, singly and in aggregate, have a blind spot when it comes to the safety net erected in the New Deal years and expanded upon in the Johnson presidency. They can't deal with it reasonably, because they learned to hate the welfare state at the

---

3   Adam Nagourney and Elizabeth Kolbert, "How Bob Dole's Dreams Were Dashed," The New York Times, November 8, 1996, p. A1. The authors note Dole finally realized that no strategy exists in September, during his debate preparations: "Mr. Dole's debate advisers sought to put him through a run of trial questions and answers, according to a participant, but the candidate cut them off: 'What I want to hear is not questions and answers: I want a strategy for winning this debate and winning this election.' Mr. Dole paused and then delivered his own verdict to his assembled staff...at the Seaview Hotel in Bal Harbour, Fla. 'We've never had a strategy for winning this election.'"

tables of their fathers and grandfathers. Establishment conservatives are essentially immobile, representing a risk-free *status quo*. To be a *movement conservative* is to belong to a much more daring bunch, who in fact want *movement*. To belong, you are required to have a quasi-religious belief, a visceral hatred of the evils of liberal social engineering, without necessarily a commensurate disdain of conservative social engineering. It was summed up in Barry Goldwater's acceptance speech of the 1964 GOP nomination: *Extremism in the defense of liberty is no vice. And...moderation in the pursuit of justice is no virtue.* The Leadership Institute's Morton Blackwell, a friend and a movement conservative with a wry sense of humor, once said: *They also serve who stand and hate.*

It is clear that if conservative Republicans ever got the kind of power that LBJ got in the 1964 election – a veto-proof majority – they would demolish the welfare state with legislative dynamite. For that reason, the American people would never give the GOP that kind of power, would not consider it a truly *national party* able to represent all the people, unless it saw in the party leadership men and women who would be kinder and gentler in unraveling the most destructive fabric of the welfare state.

Gingrich had entered the Georgia political realm as a self-styled Rockefeller Republican, especially in his advocacy of civil rights and environmental issues; he had never been a *movement* conservative. Still, he had never been a Democrat, as Reagan had been, or as the neo-conservatives who followed the political lead of Irving Kristol had been. For this reason, perhaps, he never developed the sensitivities to social spending that might have avoided his disastrous handling of the budget when, after 40 years, the people finally entrusted Congress to the GOP. Almost immediately, he was caught up in revolutionary rhetoric that turned off the electorate when it extended to closing down of government.

Could Gingrich have done it any differently? Having watched him closely, putting one foot ahead of the next as he marched his troops inexorably toward the cliff he jumped from, it was easier for me to see that it was practically his mission to see how far he could take the revolution before getting to the cliff's edge. He may have been heading in the right direction, but he was moving way too fast for the electorate. The situation was also extraordinary because we do not expect the Speaker of the House to set the nation's direction, only to correct the President's. Both friends and detractors of Gingrich commented during his worst stretches that he was acting as if he were Prime Minister, the leader who does set direction in a parliamentary system. Worse, Gingrich seemed to act as if anyone who disagreed with him did not see how marvelous his vision of where that direction would take the nation. The 14th-century Arab political philosopher, Ibn Khaldun, whom Ronald Reagan often quoted on the subject of taxation, put it like this:

> The excellence of rulership arises out of gentleness....Now it is rare to find gentleness in men who have keen intelligence and awareness; rather is it to be found among the duller people. For an intelligent ruler is apt to impose upon the subjects more than they can bear, because he sees further than they, and can, thanks to his intelligence, foresee the consequences of any act or event; all of which spells ruin to the subjects.[4]

Defeated in 1974 and 1976 in his first attempts to win a seat in Congress, and realizing his constituency was not interested in being represented by a Rockefeller Republican, Gingrich became intrigued by the supply-side economic ideas generating from *The Wall Street Journal's* editorial pages. He was also fascinated by Jack Kemp's ascendency in the House as Kemp sold the Republican Party on the idea of a 30 percent across-the-board income-tax cut – embodied in what became known as the Kemp-Roth bill. My first

---

4 Charles Issawi, *An Arab Philosophy of History: Selections from the Prolegomena of Ibn Khaldun of Tunis* (London, UK: John Murray Ltd., 1958), p. 129-130.

awareness of Gingrich came in a personal letter to me at the *Journal's* editorial page, in early 1978. It included a copy of his campaign brochure that advertised his support of Kemp-Roth, asking my opinion of how it looked. I can't recall the first time I met him face to face, after he won the seat in 1978, but he quickly became part of the circle of gladiators that fell into step behind Kemp.[5] Gingrich is best described thusly:

> Although Gingrich has changed positioning on a few issues like the environment, over a long career he has advocated steadily a coherent and consistent set of ideas. Gingrich is an American exceptionalist, a believer in the idea widely shared by American voters but widely rejected by American intellectuals that this is a uniquely good nation with a special mission in world history. While his liberal contemporaries disparaged traditional America in struggles over civil rights, he was living in the most integrated part of America, the career military, and during Vietnam he was married with children and saw no need to justify his lack of military service. Gingrich is also a believer in an energetic government that advances modern technology and promotes traditional values, a kind of American Gaullist. He is a cultural conservative who believes that liberal values are destroying the lives of the poor, a market capitalist who celebrates technological innovation.
>
> Gingrich did not gain these beliefs either from the liberals who dominated campuses when he was a young man or Congress in his later years nor from the Republicans who came to celebrate him as their deliverer. Indeed, Gingrich infuriates congressional Democrats who insist that he

---

5 The others in the group included Trent Lott of Mississippi, elected in 1972, two years after Kemp quit the Buffalo Bills and won his seat in that district. In 1982, they were joined by a young banker from Florida, Connie Mack, and a few years later by a political whiz kid from Minnesota, Vin Weber. These would all be prominent players in the 1996 election story.

believes in nothing but power (he has "an absolute ambition for power," says former Democratic leadership staffer George Stephanopoulos), though that is quite obviously wrong; he believes, whether you like them or not, in certain public policies. But the Democrats refuse to engage Gingrich's ideas: his attacks on things as they are pierce too deeply, wounding the Democrats' claims to intellectual and moral superiority, while his sloppiness in personal and political matters leaves him open to furious counterattack.[6]

In 1990, as House Minority Whip, Gingrich led the opposition to the budget deal of his party's own man in the White House, George Bush, because it raised taxes after Bush had vowed he would not do so. To raise taxes and cut spending at the same time was exactly counter to the ideas Kemp had fostered among his lieutenants and followers. In his 1979 book, *An American Renaissance*, Kemp devoted a chapter to "The Safety Net and Government Spending," which popularized the use of the term "Social Safety Net" as a way of distinguishing it from welfare dependency and a government nanny:

> The American people consider themselves a kind of extended family. I suspect it is because so many of us are descended from people who fled suffering abroad or who arrived here "down and out" that we consciously and actively seek to aid those who need our special care. We are repelled by the thought of ignoring genuine suffering.
>
> Yet because people want this safety net in place, it doesn't follow that they therefore want it filled up with sufferers. Least of all do they want their assistance to seduce others into habits of dependency. Rather, they want the type of economic expansion that will extend hope throughout the national family, supplying resources to aid those who need

---

6   Michael Barone and Grant Ujifusa, *The Almanac of American Politics 1996* (Washington, D.C.: National Journal Inc., 1995) p. 372.

our care, and opportunity to those who now accept aid but could do, and ought to be doing, otherwise.

It seems to me the proper solution to the growing burden of social spending, then, is not to lower the safety net so far that it bounces against the ground, by slashing social-support programs. Instead, we must draw people out of the net by expanding attractive opportunities in the private sector. A vibrant economy can afford to leave the safety net in place and at the same time ensure that the net is as empty as possible.[7]

Gingrich followed this careful policy path from his arrival in the House right up until his historic victory in 1994, in guiding the GOP's national effort in winning control of the House. His founding of the Conservative Opportunity Society – a Capitol Hill weekly gathering of like-minded back-benchers – established the principles by which welfare would be replaced with opportunity. It was always understood that tax cuts and economic growth would precede a downsizing of the safety net. Having been in the wilderness for so long, the Republicans presented a modest list of ten things to do should the American people give them the helm. The Contract With America, drawn up by Gingrich and a select group of advisors, with the help of a young pollster, Frank Luntz, was so modest that there was grumbling from some conservatives that it was not bold enough.

As the 104th Congress unfolded in 1995, it was not the Contract that *directly* got Gingrich and the GOP into trouble. In short order, nine of the ten items passed the House, with only the provision requiring term limits being voted down by a majority. Still, it was only promised that all ten items would be brought to a vote, which they were. The problem developed when one of the ten provisions – a call for a Constitutional amendment to require a balanced budget

---

7 Jack Kemp, *An American Renaissance: A Strategy for the 1980s* (New York, N.Y.: Harper & Row, 1979), p. 78.

– was voted down in the Senate, with one Republican, Mark Hatfield of Oregon, voting with the Democrats. A balanced-budget amendment had always been opposed by Jack Kemp on the grounds that it would have the opposite, unintended consequence of raising taxes, slowing growth, and growing bigger budget deficits. Gingrich, though, had put it in the Contract to please that faction of the GOP which would like to downsize government as soon as possible. There was no discussion with Kemp. Indeed, it is highly likely that when it was inserted in the summer of 1994, there was no serious thought that the GOP would actually win the House that November. It was assumed the Republicans would pick up seats in both House and Senate, and the Contract might help them close the gap as near as possible.

When the Senate killed the balanced-budget amendment in 1995, Newt Gingrich and Bob Dole immediately shifted gears to put a legislated balanced budget at the top of the agenda. They proposed enactment of a budget that would be in balance in the year 2002. Dropped down the priority list was Senate enactment of the tax cuts that had passed the House, including a cut in the capital gains tax which had been promised in the Contract. Gingrich did attempt to walk the narrow line between the budget balancers and tax cutters in the GOP by arguing that both be done simultaneously in the budget bill that would be sent to the President. His efforts blew up in his face when President Clinton and the Democrats developed the theme that the Republicans were cutting social spending for the needy – school lunch programs and Medicare benefits – in order to cut taxes for the rich.

By Labor Day of 1995, Congress and the President prepared for the two "train wrecks" that might be coming. The first would be a "toy train wreck," or partial shutdown of the government at the beginning of the new fiscal year on October 1, if the President did not sign any of 15 appropriation bills to continue spending on discretionary programs and would only affect paychecks for the government workers involved. The second would come November

15, when the government would run out of money for entitlement programs to pension, health and welfare recipients, unless Congress lifted the debt ceiling to permit more borrowing. Gingrich's pollster, Frank Luntz, found that 70 percent of the voters would support the GOP on the first train wreck, but only 20 percent on the second.

Had Gingrich played his cards accordingly, he might have won the public-relations battle with the President and the Democrats. This could have been done by passing the debt ceiling legislation and junking the train-wreck idea, instead sending the President appropriation bills he would have to veto and veto again until the voters saw that the Democrats were willing to shut down vital services in order to preserve pet programs that should be trimmed. On October 1, however, it became clear that Gingrich was ready to shut down the government entirely by refusing to raise the debt ceiling and have the President blamed for people not getting their welfare checks. He told the Sunday talk show, ABC's "This Week With David Brinkley," that he was not only prepared to see the government default on the national debt, but also that he expected it would be good for the bond market if that happened, because bondholders would see the government was serious about getting the deficit under control. From that moment, it seemed clear to most observers that Gingrich was viewed by the country as a menace, a man not only prepared to see the sick, the elderly and the poor hung out to dry, but also to stop payment on government bonds maturing. The Democrats wisely seized on this as a sign of GOP irresponsibility – although knowing that the Treasury Secretary could always juggle the books to make bond payments. What came through to the nation, though, was that Newt was ready to take the country over a cliff in order to get his way.

Why would Gingrich think he could get away with this gambit? As it happened, he was advised by some Wall Street big shots that he could get away with it, and *The Wall Street Journal* editorial page also encouraged him to think he could. Billionaire investor George

Soros and Stanley Druckenmiller, managing director of Soros Fund Management, advised the GOP leadership on November 1 that it was no cause for concern. A *Journal* editorial quoted Druckenmiller: "My best judgment is, if you actually got into a default, the markets would realize that anything that serious would force Congress, once they've gone down that road, and the President, to engage in a balanced budget."[8]

The government did shut down, but instead of defaulting on the debt and cutting off checks to the needy, President Clinton won all the cards on the table by using a loophole in the law to continue borrowing beyond the debt ceiling. When the dust had settled, the Republicans did not get their balanced budget in 2002, nor did they get their tax cuts. Gingrich's approval ratings in the polls were down in the low 20s where they would remain throughout the year. President Clinton had the only issue he needed for 1996. Newt Gingrich had begun his career as an unsuccessful Rockefeller liberal and transformed himself into a successful Kemp-Reagan progressive conservative to achieve his lifelong dream of becoming Speaker of the House. Then, on the first play of the game, he found himself steadily maneuvered into the corner relegated to dead and dying Hoover Republicans. The Democrats had never figured out how to beat Ronald Reagan. Hoover, they could always beat.

Gingrich's errors thus made it very difficult for Bob Dole to win the presidency, but we can just as easily say Gingrich's boldness and imagination in challenging President Bush's tax increases in 1990 and his winning the House in 1994 with the Contract With America set the stage for a GOP sweep in 1996, if only Dole had the wit to capitalize on it. In other words, for political aficionados, it is important

---

8 "The Market Bogeyman," *The Wall Street Journal* Review & Outlook, November 2, 1995, p. A18. The *Journal* editor does cite former Treasury Secretary William Simon and Former Fed Chairman Paul Volcker in opposition to the debt-limit ploy, but clearly comes down on the side of Gingrich using it, with favorable comments from Wall Street economist Ed Hyman and James Capra of Capra Asset Management, "a former Congressional Budget Office hand, [who] advised that the debt ceiling is a tried and true method of setting deadlines."

and interesting to see the cards played out exactly as they were, not to attempt "what if" scenarios. With God's help, history molds itself with the common clay with which it is provided. The party jettisons what it has to in order to accumulate the greatest amount of power, be it ideas or particular candidates. To his credit, Dole was the first to shoulder the blame for his failure to win in November, although his party did survive nicely, keeping the House of Representatives and increasing its strength in the Senate. Still, at times Dole still grumbles he might have gone all the way if it were not for Steve Forbes.

CHAPTER TWO

Enter Steve Forbes

Americans choose their Presidents the way they would build a house. At different times and different stages in the development of the nation, a different skill or talent is required. If the immediate task involves laying a foundation, the excavators are hired. Carpenters come to frame, electricians to wire, plumbers to pipe, painters to paint. It is a simple metaphor, but it's the best way I can translate the mysterious and amazing phenomenon of America's presidential elections. The national family is constantly developing a pool of political talent as little boys and little girls put themselves on paths that somehow lead to public service. Their internal energies and ideas self-select them toward higher and higher levels of elective political representation. Every four years, the electorate looks over the field of those who have presented themselves for consideration, at last winnowing out the single one whose background, talent and skill best suits the job of work at hand.

The electorate is of course limited in its selection to the available pool. The pool can theoretically expand beyond "politicians" to include anyone who fits the constitutional requirements, but it rarely needs to go beyond the professional cadre available. It obviously did so in 1992 when it pulled Ross Perot and Pat Buchanan into the arena. It did so again in 1996 when it added Steve Forbes at the last minute.

In 1994, my wife Patricia and I were invited by Jack Kemp to attend the annual conference of Empower America, which Kemp had co-founded with New York financier Ted Forstmann as a public-interest lobby in Washington, D.C., on behalf of entrepreneurial capitalism. The conference was held that September in Telluride, Colorado – where coincidentally William Jennings Bryan a hundred years earlier had first delivered what became known as his "Cross of Gold" speech, in denunciation of the gold standard. Coincidental, because I had been invited to speak on the long-standing goal of many supply-siders: to end the horrendous inflation that began when President Nixon in 1971 severed the link between the dollar and gold for the first time since 1879. In that year the United States returned to the gold standard after the Civil War greenback era, and ended the inflation it had produced.

Not all participants at the conference agreed on the need to restore some linkage between the dollar and gold, but the principals did, including Steve Forbes, the chairman of Empower America's board of trustees. Steve and I had become political friends during the previous 20 years, from the days he began appearing at supply-side gatherings and conferences as a young reporter for *Forbes*, the family business magazine. It did not take him long to become an enthusiastic advocate, even to the point of diverging from the traditional budget-balancing ideas that were held by his father, Malcolm Forbes. As Steve became more and more interested in the economic ideas that were unfolding on the editorial page of *The Wall Street Journal*, we became closer. This was primarily because we lived only 15 miles apart in northern New Jersey, he in the Far Hills horse country, I in the town of Morristown, 15 miles closer to New York City and Wall Street.

It was our quarterly breakfast meetings to talk politics and economics that cemented our political friendship, as we talked about the things going on among our other political friends as well as the world at large. As Forbes is ever the reporter, the conversation often consisted of Steve asking questions and taking notes as I rambled on over the sausage and scrambled eggs we both dished up at the buffet. It was at one such meeting that I told him I had to abandon a project I'd been working on for several years, the publication of an annual critique of the national press corps, the *MediaGuide*. One thing led to another and Steve decided to try his hand at publishing it as the

MediaCritic. My wife Patricia went along as one of the editors until he also decided it could not be sustained without perpetual subsidies.

When he knew we were both attending the same political event or GOP convention, he would invite me to fly aboard the *Capitalist Tool* with him. It was aboard that Boeing 727 that Patricia and I flew to and from the Telluride conference with Steve. Kemp, of course, spoke at the conference, as did Bill Bennett, the former Education Secretary and "Drug Czar" in the Reagan and Bush administrations, now a co-director of Empower America. The last speaker of the weekend was Steve, whose aim was to inspire the money men at the conference to serious political philanthropy on behalf of Empower America, the conservative answer to the liberal's "Common Cause." Steve spoke for no more than 30 minutes. Without a lectern or notes, he summarized the 20th century, the problems of the here and now, and how to get from here to the 21st century in a way that would restore the promise of America. I'd already considered him one of the finest speakers around, but this was a *tour de force*, and as the applause was dying down, Patricia leaned over and whispered to me, "Why don't we forget about Dole and Kemp, and run Steve for President?" It was a thought that had never crossed my mind.

On the way back to New Jersey a few hours later, we discussed Patricia's offhand remark and my belief she was right in her insight that he was potential presidential timber, a citizen politician like Ross Perot, but without Perot's angry edge. I suggested he think of the possibility that Bill Bradley, New Jersey's senior Democratic Senator, might not seek re-election in 1996, and that he could begin his journey to the White House by running for the seat, whether or not Bradley ran. I wrote the steps out on a sheet of paper or the back of an envelope, signed and dated it, and handed it over to him. From the gleam in his eye and the careful way he folded the paper and put it in his shirt pocket, there was receptivity. At the end of the trip home, though, the concept went out of my mind, returning on the morning of March 8, 1995, when I woke up thinking about it.

Enter Steve Forbes

Three days earlier, I'd decided to break off my relationship with Bob Dole. His standing in the polls had never been higher, and with President Clinton still reeling from the November 1994 election losses, the betting odds favored a Dole presidency in 1996. It was painfully frustrating for me to see him driven by the polls to political postures that the supply-siders had been struggling against for two decades. In my March 6 memo, I told him I would no longer actively work on his behalf, but would probably wind up voting for him. Still, the thought of having a presidential race without a growth candidate to at least mix it up a bit had me tossing and turning for three nights, until the seed Patricia had planted in my head the previous August germinated. Before I got out of bed, I told my wife the idea that had come to me overnight.

When I got to my office an hour later, I was astonished to find a telephone message from a reporter who wished to interview me about Steve Forbes. Louise Witt was working on a profile of Steve for the Bloomberg financial Sunday supplement. I called her immediately, agreed to the interview, and told her straight out that Steve would make a great President. The interview then proceeded along those lines, as I told her about why I thought he would make a good President, how he would govern, even the kinds of people he would appoint to his Cabinet – General Colin Powell as Secretary of State, Ted Forstmann as Secretary of the Treasury. It may have seemed a lark to Ms. Witt, but when her article appeared months later, Steve was well on his way to a run for the GOP nomination. As soon as the interview terminated, I called Steve at his office in Manhattan and told him I was getting him into trouble, that I had given the interview and the Bloomberg reporter had taken me seriously. I told him I thought he should too. His only real response was to laugh and say, "It might be fun." The very next morning, on a business trip to Hawaii, I booted up my laptop and wrote the following memo. I later faxed it to Steve from my hotel room on the island of Lanai. It was really the outline of a strategy for the year and a half ahead. The fax is key to this book, which is why I think the text should appear here in its entirety:

> [Bill] Dal Col says you are the only man he knows whose travel schedule would ease up if he ran for President. You deserve a rest, I'd say. Kemp thinks it's a great idea. So does [Ken] Tomlinson. So does Tony Snow. So does Ted Forstmann. He's the one who surprised me the most. Not a moment's hesitation when I told him I had found our candidate. Ted loves your pick for Treasury Secretary and SecState. We thought you could work yourself up to a race in 2000 and take it all in 2004. I told the Bloomberg lady you were my first choice, but I didn't think you would cut in front of Jack. Now that Jack has cut out, you are first in line anyway.
>
> John Sears believes it would be easier to nominate and elect Jack this year than it was for Nixon in '68 or Reagan in '80. This cuts entirely against the conventional wisdom, which suggests that Jack would have a hard time getting nominated with the kind of "right-wingers" who vote in GOP primaries. Sears's belief, which I of course share in spades, is that the primary voters are looking for a President who will make capitalism work at home and abroad. At the moment, the budget balancers and cultural conservatives have stolen the '94 mandate, which has pulled the center of gravity among the party elite away from the Republican electorate. The voters really don't care about the "Contract," although they do appreciate a sense of change. This, they will tire of soon if they do not get the economy moving in the right direction. There is an increasing chance the other GOP candidates – Dole, Alexander, Gramm – will lose interest in the growth aspects of the Contract as they compete for the organizational GOP voters, who do tend to be the country club variety. A giant vacuum will

open up that you can easily fill with the basic program that Jack would have gone into the campaign with, if he chose to run. There is always a slight chance Jack will toy with talking you out of the run, but I tend to think he really will choose to lay low on that score and instead become national chairman of your campaign at an appropriate moment. His role in a Forbes administration could be as chief of staff, as he has developed the skills and perspectives to integrate the legislative and executive branches. He really would be quite good at that.

The idea I presented Jack early this year was that he run a most unconventional campaign, forswearing paid TV, putting his efforts into free TV, talk shows, etc., and select paid print and radio. I thought $3 million would be enough, Sears figures $6 million, the difference probably all in paid ads. You and Dal Col have the right outfit in Chicago to develop what little you might need. Mostly, we would hammer together a "Contract with the World." A program of 10 steps that would ready the United States for its primary leadership role of the 21st Century. You would run as a citizen of the world, and have people around the planet cheering for you in the primaries. On this Sears emphatically agreed with me on Jack, and would do so even more so with you, I would imagine. The concept is to run as an internationalist *in a way that attracts the nationalists.* A representative of progressive conservatism, entrepreneurial capitalism, and populist democracy.

You start with a great name, Malcolm Forbes, known at least as well and probably more than Ross Perot at the time of his entry in February '92. You actually have a lead of 11 months on Ross. And remember, he did not spend more than pocket money from the moment he indicated he would run if the country wanted him to run, and the day he hit 40 percent in a matchup with Bush and Clinton. The initial hesitancy I get from supply-siders when I bring up your candidacy is your "shyness," your outward demeanor. Your ability to speak with extemporaneous skill, in measured tones and the compactness of a self-edited writer, is unparalleled among conservatives. Reagan had more style, the ability to more easily connect with the common man, than you do, but your range of information is far greater than his, and you have the advantage of standing on his shoulders. Jack has more energy in his presentations than you do and will get more spontaneous applause lines, but your messages tend to be philosophically seamless and appealing. I remember listening to one of the tapes of the Armstrong Williams show that you appeared on, thinking how easily you connect with black intellectuals and ordinary folk.

What would of course come across throughout is the sense that you are as comfortable in your own skin as Reagan, far more so than Jack, who will be deviled by insecurities into his '90s. This is most important as to the why you are seeking the presidency. I told the Bloomberg lady that the only reason you would run is that you believed you would be a better President at this moment of our nation's history than the other candidates in the field. You would not run if Jack were, because it is not clear to you that you would be superior. If the nation has need of a Bob Bennett [of Utah] to leave his business at age 59 and run for the U.S. Senate, to impart his knowledge and experience with entrepreneurial capitalism, it is enough to draw him into the political realm, and win against all political advice and conventional prognostication. I've actually thought of Bob as a potential presidential contender in '96 for that reason, and Dick Fox and I, who have been kicking this around for several years, have believed that the man elected President in '96 would be someone who surfaced out of the blue. Bennett is not quite right, not comfortable with the idea that he may be the man of the hour, and he will serve the nation best by remaining in the Senate for the moment. He is more or less Dole's man, although not an entirely happy one either.

It would certainly be clear to ordinary voters in any debate situation that you would stand above the rest of the field in terms of your scope. The "message" and the "vision" that everyone talks about are attempts to categorize "a certain something" that eludes us until we see it. Lamar Alexander is in the race because he "feels" it "out there," perhaps from his treks across Tennessee. His limitations are so far apparent in the people he has assembled around him to "manage" his campaign. His "feel" for the electorate will not be enough for him to rise above his handlers, though. None of them have the deep sense of the American family – by which I mean all of us in our nation – and how it yearns to be made whole. If it is not on your mind or close to being on your mind all the time, it will be transparent to the electorate that it is not something you put near the top of your list of concerns. If you don't have this sense of national family, you will not be able to convey a sense of international family. There could be no "Contract with the World." It wouldn't ring true. Bob Dole really lost me last week when he spoke on foreign policy at the Nixon Center, and described the Russians as our "rivals," with a "national interest" that does not square with ours. We can in fact have rivalries within families, but they are natural and healthy, as with "sibling rivalries," which is not where Dole is coming from. His war experience is a constant reminder at his right side of a defensiveness that may cause him to see enemies where there are none. It is useful to have such people nearby, but this is not the moment of our history where we should be choosing fights with relatives who have recently conceded defeat. You can appreciate that, somehow, perhaps because of your worldliness, a natural gentleness that you inherited from your parents that is most appropriate in times like these. A kinder, gentler Perot?

Remember my Perot paper of '92, when I thought he could win it all? I spoke of the electorate as if it were a rough diamond that would cleave into gems if struck just so, but would shatter into glass if hammered at the wrong angle. If you first decide what it is the electorate wants, and then arrange all your ideas and energies to that end, the diamond would cleave. An expression of just what it is the nation wants is most important so that the nation can nudge you during the campaign toward refinements. The electorate will also test you to see how far you are willing to "refine" a vision. If you depart from the central sense of where they are, the voters will know you will in the end not be confident enough in your own program to fight for it. In other words, the electorate cannot sense in you a rigidity of direction that causes you to crash when there is a sudden turn in the road, nor can you exhibit a rubberiness that suggests you will depart from the correct path on a whim.

For a man without a track record in politics, your biggest deficiency is the electorate's sense that no matter how good you may appear on the surface, you may crack under pressure. The campaign itself is plenty of pressure, but the electorate will want more than that from a neophyte. The world is too dangerous a place and civilization has come too far to put an untested leader at the helm of the only superpower. Perot cracked under this kind of pressure. I warned him to his face in March '92 that the establishment would attempt to destroy him, even with real bullets perhaps, because of his independent candidacy. The testing you would go through would be of a different kind, as you would enter through the normal party system and would not drop from the sky so suddenly. How do you offset the amount of testing that will be necessary to get to the pot of gold at the end of the rainbow? You first put together a team that knows that curves in the road will be coming and will be able to alert you. Perot's choice of Ed Rollins caused him to get run over by a Mack truck in the first week of the relationship, if you will recall. The political establishment of course first will examine the people around you and study their weaknesses, as a way of testing yours. If you have people like Jack with you, up front, and Christie Whitman perhaps, and a few supply-side governors who do not like the present field, and see you as the true Reaganaut, you will develop a critical mass early on. Not next week, of course. You would have to demonstrate in a few speeches to the Detroit and New York economic clubs that you will be a blessing and credit to the establishment as well as the populace – that you above all understand *pace and timing* in the elaboration of an agenda. Our gang has enough early firepower to get you a serious hearing. The earliest commentary will of course be that you are not really serious, but are a stalking horse for someone else, or, better yet, a supply-side voice that will force the other contenders to move in our direction. This may in fact be the way it turns out, of course, although the whole point of this missive is to point up the likelihood of a surprise victory. Wendell Wilkie did get the nomination for the GOP in 1940 as a One World Republican candidate, but we were then headed into war, and the electorate could not risk a neophyte businessman-politician. We are now headed out of war, which is why the symmetry holds for you.

The conventional wisdom now suggests the GOP nomination will be issueless, fought out over personalities, because all the candidates are more or less in the same mold. They all want to balance the budget, deregulate, devolve, get family values back in town. Etc. This laundry list is all the result of the professional pollsters trolling up and down the coasts and delving into the interior. I would actually announce up front that I would not take any polls. Lincoln didn't. Teddy Roosevelt didn't. Calvin Coolidge wouldn't spend a dime on one. (You absolutely must read Charles Beard's "Republic," ASAP. He has a devastating section on the evils of public opinion polls as a substitute for leadership.) Lamar has told people he would not use Armey's flat tax, as it has not done well in the polls. Mike Murphy, his media man, ran unsuccessfully with the flat tax in N.J. with Haytaian. I might not recommend you do Armey's flat tax either, as we may have a better idea. The electorate is not as interested in the mechanics of taxation in a candidate as in his sense of daring. Dole will always lose on that count. Reagan gambled that the people would respond to incentives. So did Maggie Thatcher. The crowd we have running for President are risk averse budget-balancers. Even Dick Armey shies from cutting tax rates without offsetting spending cuts, with all his talk of dynamic analysis.

It would be your flair for discussing reforms with broad brushes that would make you credible, your father's son in a hot air balloon reaching for pie in the sky. You could promise that in your first 100 hours you would index capital gains across the board through executive order, fix the price of gold at $350 an ounce through executive order, lift all economic embargoes through executive order – including Iraq, Korea, Cuba, Libya, while declaring a clean slate for the 21st century. You could also declare amnesty for various types of non-violent criminals (something to cut against the Willie Horton bias in the GOP) and say you will restore Mike Milken's citizenship.[1] In the campaign, you could also pledge to support a constitutional amendment for initiative and referenda – a pro-democracy amendment as opposed to term-limits and BBA [Balanced Budget Amendment]. You would preserve the social safety net, but tighten means testing in accord with economic expansion. That is, you would design a system that becomes more generous in bad times and less generous in good times. Once you have in your head that the electorate wants more political freedom, more avenues to express collective wisdom, you will have no trouble maintaining a consistency of vision.

Unconventional campaign? Sears would have most of the good ideas on that score. I'm arranging for him to meet with John Engler on March 23, when Engler will be in DC, as Engler is my favorite governor. A Forbes-Engler ticket? Almost certainly you will want a big state governor as your running mate, as this is where the action will be in Newt's continuing devolution. Because of the configuration of the primaries, it is now quite possible that there will not be a winner after California. This is now the thesis of Bob Merry, editor of *CQ*, who believes the field will be so big come '96 that candidates will focus their energies on different states, and there will be a brokered convention. Whatever the case, the notion of an unconventional cut-rate campaign will soon replace the conventional idea that it requires $25-$30 million to run in '96 and that only Dole, Gramm and Alexander will be viable. Engler cannot really take on the presidential campaign because he is immersed

---

1 Forbes and I were both ardent fans of Milken as a financier of entrepreneurial capitalists and had come to believe in his innocence even after he was imprisoned on felony counts to which he pled guilty, believing it was useless to fight the corporate Establishment and the federal government. Of course, Milken did not lose his citizenship. I simply meant Steve could give him a full pardon.

in governing, has a wife with new triplets, and is not seasoned outside of the realm of local governance. He would falter quickly against Dole's presence or the organizations of Gramm and Alexander. As your running mate, he would immediately give weight and depth to your campaign. The mere fact that he would agree to run with you from the get-go would impress the hell out of the political establishment, and impress the hell out of the governors. They would see in this combine a fighting team of business/governance in the Reagan mold, with the supply-siders firmly behind it. Christie Whitman would endorse the ticket vigorously, and you would begin the campaign with New Jersey and Michigan in your bag, the equivalent of California. What I am saying here is that Engler is most likely to pass on a national campaign if he is to head the ticket, but would relish being No. 2 to you, as it would permit him to campaign for the nomination from his desk in Lansing, lining up the governors for you. If you and he came out of the box in May or June, as a unit, with Jack designated the national chairman, you can already imagine the clout you would enjoy. It would make you credible, which is all you need to start with.

My guess is that you could raise sufficient funds with the announcement that you will limit your own contribution to $1,000, with another $1,000 from Sabina, et cetera. George Washington didn't have $6 million, nor did Abe Lincoln. This can't be seen as a money grab by a Forbes rich kid, on Lifestyles of the Rich and Famous. Perot didn't have that problem because of his personal diplomacy in Vietnam and a general awareness that he made his billions from the ground up. Jerry Brown limited his contributions to $100, as I recall, but there is no reason to be cute. Play within the rules. You can always lend yourself a stake, but make it clear you expect to be able to persuade ordinary people to contribute if they wish to see you elected. As a Scot, you can promise to issue reports on how you are spending their money, making it clear that not one dime is going to pay for polling or TV soundbites. Once you pledge that executive order to index capgains retroactively, the dollars will come in from everywhere, from the farmers and ranchers and small businessmen who are now cornered.

You would be free to run a liberated type of political campaign, one that would not require you to bash your opponents. You are always free to criticize an opponent publicly, though, by way of telegraphing information about yourself. Dole should be criticized for being too rigid in his approach to the Balkans, too quick to threaten force. Gramm should be criticized for being too quick to cut spending, to zero-out federal social programs with a meat ax instead of a scalpel. Alexander should be criticized for his heavy reliance on pollsters. Downsizing is the national will, as part of the return to normalcy. But it is all in the timing. You don't burn down an old house before you build a new one. Don't even allow yourself to think of your campaign as a "tax-cutting campaign," but rather as a campaign to bring about a rebirth of the nation and fulfill the Gipper's vision of the "City on a Hill," a beacon for the rest of humanity.

On race, you clearly state your objective, to have half of all black Americans voting Republican by the year 2000 – the young men and women who are eager for enterprise and capitalism, while you promise to be careful with their parents and grandparents who look to the government for security and assistance – even while knowing they will probably not be able to trust you and will vote Democratic. Be honest and discard the idea that we should be a color-blind society in this hour and at this time. That is the promised land to which we aspire, but until we get there, we should all be honest with ourselves and say there is racism that burdens our black brothers and sisters. With Forbes in the White House, Armstrong Williams will be RNC chairman!

On national defense and security, you are the iron fist in the velvet glove. There is a Star Wars in our future, and a space program, and the economic expansion that will occur as a result of your economic program will provide the resources for these even while moving toward budget equilibrium. Your first option is always diplomacy. You will make it plain that if you are President, you will not take no for an answer from Colin Powell as Secretary of State, Ted Forstmann at Treasury, Jack as chief of staff or at the World Bank or at Empower America, Dave McCurdy at Defense perhaps. Pick your key Cabinet people up front, which is the quickest way you can signal to the electorate the shape of your thinking and make them comfortable with your lack of political credentials. A Dole will be reluctant to do this because he is not confident that his choice will be the right one in terms of winning the nomination. He is more likely to run the kind of campaign that attempts to put together a coalition of states. You should run your campaign as if you were running for the Democratic nomination for President, and allow your competitors to divide up the organization Republicans. You will then win the masses of ordinary Republicans who have been waiting for someone to unify the nation. Do you own a stovepipe hat?

6 pm, Honolulu time

The next day Steve called from Florida to tell me he and Sabina had read the memo and had been *"bowled over"* by it. While he had been amused by my phone call, he said he would now have to give my memo serious consideration. His only point of disagreement was on my suggestion that he run a campaign conventionally financed by money raisers. He said that George Washington believed that if you are blessed by both talent and treasure, you should be willing to use both on behalf of your country. We agreed to get together as soon as we both returned to New Jersey.

It certainly seemed to me the only real contender who had any chance to take the nomination from Dole was Steve. With Kemp out of the race, he was the only one of the 11 GOP candidates who began the race to represent the party's economic growth wing – as opposed to its austerity wing, its social conservatives, or its social liberals. It was on that basis that a number of Reaganauts in the GOP's growth wing finally persuaded him to run. He came into the field with the sunniest issues, "hope, growth and opportunity." These were propelled by fundamental economic reforms, chiefly the flat-tax idea, rapid non-inflationary growth, and a populist end to corruption of Washington insiders. At one point, his message seemed to catch fire at the grass roots, as he led in the tracking polls in New Hampshire and the betting odds against him in London dropped sharply, getting as low as 7 to 2. His fatal flaw proved to be the same as Dole's, only more so. With no experience in elective politics, the 47-year-old magazine publisher chose as his campaign manager a man who had only slightly more experience in political campaigns than Scott Reed. Steve never seemed to believe he needed a political strategy, believing his superior ideas would attract voters like bees to honey. All he thought he needed was someone to manage his schedule and spend as much money as it took to get the message out. He chose Bill Dal Col, a young man 10 years his junior with a bit of experience in campaigns, but none in presidential politics. Ironically, Scott Reed and Dal Col were friends who had worked for Jack Kemp when he was Secretary of Housing and Urban Development in the Bush administration. The two even continued to communicate during the heat of battle.

Forbes had chosen as campaign manager Dal Col, an amiable fellow who, like Reed, could function as an administrator. Steve had come to know and trust him when the two worked together at Empower America. I had argued strenuously for John Sears, a political veteran and one of those who encouraged Forbes to get into the race, believing he could go all the way. The exact opposite of a nuts-and-bolts campaign manager, a strategist *par excellence*, Sears was the most experienced field general in presidential politics available in the Republican Party. Had Kemp decided to run, he would have chosen Sears as strategist, with Dal Col handling the day to day management, the "nuts and bolts," as we referred to mechanical aspects of a campaign. Sears is the man I believe deserves *most* of the credit for Ronald Reagan winning the GOP nomination in 1980, having persuaded Reagan in 1979 to join forces with Jack Kemp and the nascent growth wing of the GOP. In 1987, when Kemp was deciding who would manage his 1988 run for the White House, he was talked out of Sears in favor of Charlie Black, who had been Sears's lieutenant in Reagan's 1980 race for the nomination. Sears was so sure Kemp could win the presidency in 1996 that in January 1995, he had flown to Florida, where Kemp was attending the Super Bowl, to try one last time to persuade Jack to run for the GOP nomination.[2] It turned out that Jack had already made up his mind and informed his family he would retire from elective politics. On his return from Florida, he called a press conference and announced he would not run. Sears told me Clinton would be re-elected, that the voters would never put Dole in the White House, and we might as well bide our time until 2000.

After Steve told me he would seriously consider a run, I immediately called Sears and told him I thought we had a candidate. Before anyone could get serious about Steve's candidacy, including Steve himself, it was clear to me Sears should meet with him, size him up and evaluate his chances. In early April, he flew from Washington to

---

2 Kemp cited the enormous cost of running, at a time he still had not retired his campaign debts from his unsuccessful 1988 run for the GOP nomination. Privately, Kemp also believed his party had moved far to his right on the cultural issues, lengthening the odds against his winning.

New York and met with Steve for two hours. Deciding Steve was serious, he told me the candidacy was worth exploring. Sears and I both assumed that if he did run, Sears would run the campaign. Who else could? It would give the candidacy instant credibility. Steve, though, opened up another option. His good friend Ken Tomlinson, former director of the Voice of America and in 1995 the president of the Reader's Digest Association, recommended he meet with Tom Ellis and Carter Wren of North Carolina, political operatives who had been close to Jesse Helms. Tomlinson and Steve had gotten to know Helms while gaining his support for the Voice of America. I'd met Ellis and Wren when they worked as minor consultants to the Kemp campaign during 1987 and 1988. Ellis, the senior partner in that partnership, was widely credited in 1976 with rescuing Ronald Reagan from national political oblivion by helping him win the North Carolina primary. Ellis did so at the point when the Reagan effort to wrest the GOP nomination away from President Gerald R. Ford was on the rocks. He did so by raising funds for a half-hour paid TV address by Reagan that turned the tide.

If Reagan had lost North Carolina, he may well have dropped out of the race and out of politics for good, but the win was followed by others, down to the wire. Ellis and others blamed Sears for dropping the ball at the eleventh hour by choosing a liberal Senator, Richard Schweiker of Pennsylvania, as Reagan's running mate. For this reason, Ellis and Wren, good ol' boys of the right, had an intense dislike for John Sears, a worldly fellow with scarcely concealed contempt for them. Just as Kemp was forced to decide between Sears and Black in 1988, Forbes was at a fork in the road, Sears or Ellis. Temporizing, he thought he could resolve the conflict by naming his brother Tim as the campaign's overseer. Including Tim and Dal Col, the weight of opinion among Steve's friends on who should run things came down decisively on the side of Ellis and Wren, which really meant Wren, who wound up dominating the management of the campaign from Forbes headquarters in Bedminster, New Jersey. After months of agonizing, Forbes rejected Sears along with the strategy Sears had designed in a lengthy memo which I thought testified to Sears's brilliance – one that rejected hand-to-hand combat with the professional politicians in the race. It was his idea that Steve should present a totally positive set of ideas on how to manage the nation and the world, overwhelming the establishment forces with the confidence of his platform instead of through a series of duels.

Forbes rejected Sears partly because he was uncomfortable with Sears himself, partly because he doubted he would get very far with Sears as his campaign manager. In the first major meeting we had in Steve's office to discuss the possibilities of his candidacy, Sears talked non-stop for an hour as if to persuade the several people in the room that he knew more than all of us. Steve is the most taciturn of men, in private conversation seldom stringing together more than two or three sentences. He was taken aback by Sears's filibuster, which led him to readily accept the argument from Ellis, Wren & Co., that Sears would brook no interference from anyone, including Steve, if he were hired to execute the lofty plan he had designed. Forbes was prepared to spend a slice of his fortune on his candidacy, which he made clear at that first meeting, but he wanted to maintain control himself. He finally settled on giving Dal Col the title of campaign manager. Dal Col, though, decided to travel with the candidate, which ceded effective power over the campaign to the number one man at headquarters, Carter Wren, a movement conservative with a taste for negative campaigning and the jugular.

Steve somehow managed to persuade himself that he could proceed with a team that had never operated at the level of a presidential campaign, one whose stock in trade was negative advertising, a concept antithetical to his life and personae. Forbes had scarcely thought of running for public office before 1995, let alone the presidency. He had tens of millions of dollars to spend on a learning curve, however. It was simply much easier to be as comfortable as possible with the people around him, whatever their experience, and trust in the power of his ideas. The really big idea was a fundamental tax reform of the kind House Majority Leader Dick Armey had put into legislative form – a single income tax rate of 17 percent with personal exemptions that would eliminate the income tax altogether for a family of four with $35,000 in gross income. At first, it seemed as if the prairie fire he began with his "flat tax" candidacy might be all he needed. Here was a kinder and gentler Ross Perot, offering himself as a citizen candidate the way Wendell Wilkie did successfully in coming out of the private sector in 1940, with no political experience, to snatch the GOP nomination and at one point appear to be leading President Franklin D. Roosevelt in the polls. Indeed, one of the devices I used to persuade Steve to run was to send him a book about the 1940 race and argue that the only thing that kept Wilkie from the Oval Office was the advent of war, and FDR's argument that you should not change horses in midstream.

There was a point at which I thought Steve might have been right after all. Sears never wavered in his belief that Forbes was going to be taught an expensive lesson in world-class politics. At the peak of Forbes's run, when he was simultaneously on the cover of *Time* and *Newsweek* but before any votes had actually been cast, Sears looked over the chessboard and told me that the Forbes balloon was about to burst. Forbes had no strategy, except making uplifting speeches at Rotary clubs about the flat tax while spending part of his fortune, perhaps as much as $37 million, on negative TV spots designed by Carter Wren and young pollster John McLaughlin to tear down Dole's lead. Forbes was not prepared for the ground attack that came at him from Dole's support in the Christian Coalition and the GOP organization. Steve's big lead in the Iowa poll a week before the caucuses evaporated when the Coalition foot soldiers began making thousands of phone calls every day, informing church members that Forbes was *pro-abortion* – a falsehood. Steve's position was only slightly different than the consensus at the Christian Coalition. It wasn't a nice thing for Christians to do, but it got the job done. Having dismissed warnings that he needed his own ground troops to counter Dole's among Iowa's religious right, Forbes barely survived in Iowa.[3] Then, his lead in New Hampshire evaporated when the Dole campaign blanketed the state with fraudulent negative TV spots aimed at Forbes, delivered by the popular Republican Governor Steve Merrill. Forbes got no sympathy in arguing that the Merrill spots were based on false information, as his own spots designed by Carter Wren had flagrantly stretched the truth about Dole's record. Early in 1995, Kemp had promised to support Forbes's candidacy, but then backed away on the grounds that he disagreed with Forbes's use of negative ads against Dole. When Steve finally promised to stop running the ads, largely to win Kemp's endorsement, the race was essentially over. By coming to Steve's aid at that last minute, though, Kemp rescued himself in the eyes of his supply-side allies, who may have never forgiven him if he had watched Steve sink without so much as an offer of a helping hand. The gutsy move restored Kemp as the leader of the growth wing of the Republican party instead of a retired party elder. Dole would eventually realize this in asking Jack to join the ticket.[4]

To the end of his life, Dole will probably blame Forbes for having upset his game plan and perhaps even causing his defeat in November by weaking his hold over primary voters. Simply by entering the race, though, Forbes unquestionably had changed its dynamics and the course of history. His almost single-minded focus was on the flat-tax reform that he said would at one and the same time dramatically propel the economy to higher levels of economic growth and lift the intrusiveness of government from the daily lives of the American people. He essentially wrenched the debate away

---

3 In the March 1 newsletter cited in Chapter One, I noted: "As an untested political leader, Steve Forbes came into the race with more question marks than Buchanan, as far as the *institution* was concerned. He has to prove his worth, through trials of fire, before party leaders can make the calculation that he is at least as safe as Dole or [former Tennessee Gov. Lamar] Alexander," who was the organization's second choice after Dole.

4   Jude Wanniski, "Dole-Kemp Ticket Now in Play," Polyconomics, Inc., Morristown, N.J., August 8, 1996.

from how fast either party could balance the budget to a debate on taxes and economic growth. Largely due to the growth campaign Forbes ran, the Dow Jones Industrial Average hit 6000 during the year[5] as the market celebrated the move from budget balancing to tax reform and growth. The Forbes run also brought Kemp back into line for the Republican presidency in 2000. If Jack did make the run and Forbes decided to back him instead of challenge, Steve would still be young enough to run for governor of New Jersey in 2001 and get to the White House while in his 60s. At the very least, another ball had been put into play.

---

5 Jude Wanniski, "Forbes on the Move," Polyconomics, Inc., Morristown, N.J., January 31, 1996.

The Simple Democratic Strategy

A n incumbent can actually lay down a strategy and announce it openly, as the Clinton team did, because it is engaged almost entirely in strategic *defense*. That is, the team wants the voters to know that its entire plan is to defend the country against the bad guys who are trying to take it over. If it is going to tell the country that is its strategy, it cannot keep the information from the bad guys. Dole, Reed and his team thus knew the Clinton game plan from the beginning. They were told that the President would warn the voters that if Dole were elected, he and Gingrich would conspire next January to balance the budget on the backs of the masses. And they would do so in order to give tax breaks to people who are well off. They would scare the voters who rely on Medicare and other forms of government income redistribution. This defensive strategy had a key second line of defense, which was that the President would satisfy the concerns of those who might rally to the Dole forces. Clinton would have a tax cut that would be smaller than Dole's, and thus be more responsible, which would enable him to preserve Medicare.

This defensive strategy was eminently credible, because of the way Newt Gingrich and his House revolutionaries mismanaged the 10-point Contract With America in the 104th Congress. The mismanagement was not entirely due to Republican tactical errors, however. The polls had scarcely closed and the GOP celebrations begun when the Democrats were already pondering ways to slow the GOP's momentum when the new Congress opened in January of 1995. Dick Morris would later take and be given most of the credit for turning the tide with his shrewd advice to the embattled

The Simple Democratic Strategy

President. Months before Morris got into the act with his tactical ideas on how the President should give the Republicans the rope with which they would hang themselves, Michael Kinsley was designing the basic strategy and posting it on the editorial page of *The New York Times*,[1] which is practically a bulletin board for the Democratic Party's intellectuals.

An intellectual, not a political soldier, Michael Kinsley, then editor of *The New Republic*, was clearly the ablest of the political theoreticians in the Democratic Party. A week after his party's stunning defeat at the polls, Kinsley advised that the Democrats give Gingrich everything he wanted in the Contract With America, with the sole exception of its promise to cut the capital gains tax to 15 percent from 28 percent. At all costs, Kinsley wrote, Democrats should prevent that terrible thing from happening. Give Newt a balanced-budget amendment, welfare reform, line-item veto, devolution of power from federal to state government, etc., but fight to the death to prevent item Number Ten in the Contract from being enacted. The importance of the op-ed cannot be underestimated, because it not only held out a plan for an orderly, strategic retreat, but gave the demoralized troops an idea of where to draw the line. This piece turned out to be the general strategy that was followed by the White House and Democrats.

> President Clinton is getting a lot of free advice about how to deal with Tuesday's election disaster. Most of it is telling him to abandon his left-wing agenda and rediscover the inner moderate who propelled him to victory in 1992. Bipartisan accommodation should be his goal, it is said. This isn't completely wrong, but here are three problems with it.
>
> First, the notion that Mr. Clinton ran as a moderate 'new Democrat' and then has governed as some kind of McGovernite left-winger is mostly the product of

---

1 Michael Kinsley, "Play Nice, Play Tough," *The New York Times*, November 13, 1994, p. E15.

Republican agitprop and lazy journalists' shorthand. The most familiar items in the indictment – his top-bracket tax increase, his proposal to overhaul the health care system, homosexuals in the military – were all things he clearly promised in the campaign.

The tax increase affected a tiny fraction of the population; 10 times as many have enjoyed a tax cut, through expansion of the earned income tax credit. The health care autopsy will go on forever, but Mr. Clinton's original plan, whatever its flaws, was not the standard left-wing proposal for a Canadian-style Government takeover. And Mr. Clinton (not to his credit) tried mightily to fudge and postpone and compromise the gay-troops issue; it was the opposition that mischievously made it Issue One of the new administration...

A second problem with the moderate, accommodationist strategy is that it wouldn't really give voters much reason to vote for Mr. Clinton in 1996. It would leave Republicans in charge of the agenda and leave Mr. Clinton to be perceived as a whiny supplicant, not a strong leader. Republicans will quite reasonably ask the voters, 'If you like the last two years better than Bill Clinton's first two, why not finish the cleanup job?' Even if the Democratic President and the Republican Congress work well together, Mr. Clinton will be reduced to building his re-election campaign around the boring theme that divided government is best. And besides being boring, it contradicts what he said last time.

A third problem with a govern-from-the-center strategy is that the 'center' these days is mostly a land of alchemy, where it is easy to campaign but hard to govern.

It is a place where taxes can be cut and budgets balanced without any impositions on treasured government benefits of the middle class. It is a place where health care can be extended to the uninsured without raising anyone's bill, and prices can be brought under control without curtailing anyone's freedom of choice.

On foreign policy, it is a place where America can stand tall as the world's leader, and strut as the promoter of democracy and human rights, but American blood and treasure need never be spent in any particular situation.

The politics of the free lunch, which Mr. Reagan introduced into fiscal policy in 1980, now dominate in every sphere. Being a 'centrist' means mostly taking the pleasant stuff from both sides of the traditional debate and leaving out the unpleasant stuff. Both parties play this game. Mr. Clinton played it well enough to get elected in 1992. But surely one lesson of the 1994 election results is that Republicans – who invented it – will always play it better. The only hope for the Democrats is to wean the voters from the free lunch and force them to make an honest choice about what they want their Government to do and how they propose to pay for it.

So yes, President Clinton should join in at least some of the Republicans' agenda. But less in the spirit of accommodation than in the spirit of challenge – calling their bluff, holding their feet to the fire. This is, among other advantages, a way to appear both feistily 'Trumanesque' and becomingly 'moderate' at the same time. Republicans have indeed managed to occupy the center of American politics. But the goal should be to kick them out, not just to join them there.

The G.O.P.'s 'Contract With America,' with its impossible combination of tax cuts and spending increases and balanced-budget promises, offers the perfect vehicle for such a challenge.

The promise of a balanced budget (by the year 2002) alone will require something like a trillion dollars of spending cuts, even before the document's other goodies are paid for. During the campaign, the Republicans swore they could achieve this without reducing Social Security or Medicare benefits.

It can't be done, of course. That's why Mr. Clinton should give them every opportunity to try. He shouldn't 'cooperate.' His line should be: After you, Alphonse. Ronald Reagan's mantra – repeated thousands of time by Republican politicians – was that Government spending is not the President's responsibility, because under the Constitution 'Congress appropriates every dime.'

Fine, Mr. Clinton should say. Appropriate away. But give me that line-item veto you're always carrying on about, in case I notice some wasteful spending around Marietta, Ga. (home of the new House Speaker).

To keep up the pressure, the President should endorse the balanced budget amendment. The year 2002 will be more than two decades after the Reagan mega-deficit began, and 12 years after the much-maligned Bush 1990 budget deal started us back toward fiscal sanity. Although there is no real reason the budget needs to be balanced in any particular year, it was never anyone's idea of Keynesianism that the Government should spend more than it takes in every year, indefinitely.

True, it is a pity to clutter up the Constitution. But an acknowledgment by the majority that it is unable to restrain itself through normal democratic procedures is arguably just the sort of thing that does belong there. Mr. Clinton should also endorse term limits, or at least say he has no objection to them...

Not everything in the Republican Contract is beneficial or meaningless. But after outflanking the opposition on one or two fronts, and by choosing his battles carefully, Mr. Clinton could score some mighty victories. Do the Republicans, for example, really want to push a big new tax cut for the rich by expanding the capital gains tax break? I hope so. And if they try to tie it to a broader tax cut for the middle class, that would be a perfect occasion for Clinton to demand the line-item veto they promised in their Contract.

The strategy I'm advocating here might be called 'confrontational accommodationism' or 'in-your-face-moderation.' It might not work. But does anybody have a better idea?

The op-ed worried me the moment I saw it. Kinsley did not write this as a private memo to the President, but as an idea he knew would tempt the budget-balancers in the GOP. *Mr. President, let's give Gingrich nine out of ten of what he asked in the Contract, but fight him tooth and nail on his tenth demand – tax cuts for the rich to pay for the balanced budget.* The correct response from Newt was to insist upon Number Ten as the first item of business in the Congress, in order to expand the economy and make the other Nine more palatable to people who were being frightened about Medicare. By putting economic growth at the top of the agenda instead of balancing-the-budget, those tens of millions of Americans who worry about skinflint Republicans would be mollified. This is not Monday morning quarterbacking, but my advice at the time. Two days after Kinsley's op-ed appeared, I wrote a memo to the four top GOP leaders – Newt Gingrich, Bob Dole, House Majority Leader Dick Armey, and Senate Majority Whip Trent Lott.

The exit polls showed 78 percent of the voters said the elections were against the Democratic agenda and only 18 percent said they were for the GOP agenda. There was no mandate for a GOP agenda, merely a mandate for a change in direction. As I put it:

[T]he voters do not want to go Northeast, over a cliff, but it is not clear they want to go Southeast or Southwest or Northwest. Our chief mission in the next two years is to find that direction and build a GOP case for traveling there. I want to get where you guys want to get, to the land of milk and honey, and I think the American people do too, but by which route? And at what pace? That is, do we shoot the wounded in order to make better time? My best advice is that while trying to do as much as possible, try to get at least one thing done for sure that lifts the spirits of the country and makes those people who voted Republican feel like their investment paid off. You will then persuade them to double-up in '96 and bring their uncles and aunts with them. The only thing that I know will do that for sure is to cut the capital gains tax and index it retroactively, which will instantly wipe tax liabilities off $7 trillion in inflated values – and liquefy this amount of capital. If we could have persuaded Bush to do this by executive order in '92, the voters would have forgiven him his read-my-lips fiasco. Remember why Reagan was so effective and so loved. Unlike the fox, who knows everything but accomplishes little, Reagan was the hedgehog, who knows one thing and gets it done.[2]

Although Dole was the senior leader in the GOP and the front-runner for the presidential nomination, Gingrich was clearly in charge of the legislative agenda by virtue of having led the party to control of the House of Representatives for the first time in 40 years. There was no hesitation from Gingrich in *acting* that role, not even making a pretense of conferring with the Senate leader before making grand pronouncements of timing and strategy on party objectives. Almost in awe, Dole stood aside and watched. Had Gingrich in those early moments chosen to put the tax cuts and economic

---

2 Jude Wanniski, Memo to GOP leaders, November 15, 1994.

growth at the top of the agenda, there could be no doubt, then or now, that he would have had the President cornered. To have been so ignominiously rejected by the voters, Bill Clinton at that moment neither had the stomach nor the sense to resist. Had he done so, he could never have recovered in the eyes of the electorate by later developing arguments that the tax cuts would have to be paid for by cutting social services.

It was not as if Gingrich and the Republicans had not gone around this track before. When President Bush was elected in his 1988 landslide, the only specific economic idea he had campaigned on was the same reduction in the capital gains tax that Gingrich in 1994 put in the Contract. Bush could have sent that single proposal up as HR 1, the first legislation to be considered, and asked for its immediate passage.

Instead, Newt saw an opportunity to make history by grabbing the Nine items in the Contract. He would then, flushed with triumph, come back to get Number Ten. The rest is conventional history. Newt got a few small victories and cut a few billion from the trillion-dollar federal budget. In a more significant win, he got the President to sign welfare-reform legislation, but in a way that enabled the President to say, with crocodile tears, *Gingrich and Dole made me do it, but if you vote for me on November 5, I'll come back and fix it so you don't starve.*

The political cost of winning these victories was much higher than Gingrich had supposed, but certainly not so high that the losses could not be recouped in the 1996 elections. The GOP simply had to find a way to assure the nation that it had learned its lesson, that it realized it had put the cart before the horse in trying to downsize the federal government before first expanding the economy. Any strategy based on any other principle would inevitably fail. In absolving themselves of blame in the loss of the presidency, those Republicans who encouraged the Gingrich assault on federal spending blame the President for "scaring the American people." But it was Gingrich and his wild-eyed revolutionaries who did the scaring. Michael Kinsley had set forth the general strategy of "confrontational accommodationism," as he called it, "in-your-face moderation."

Dick Morris, a switch-hitting political consultant who had counseled Republican candidates, including Trent Lott, knew the President need only be *a little bit less conservative* than the Republicans. The heart of his advice was that Mr. Clinton should show the electorate that he was willing to accommodate its wishes by moving in the new direction set by Newt Gingrich, *but not as fast*. It was the Kinsley strategic idea that was the key, the idea that ultimately triumphed – holding back the capital gains tax cut in the Contract on the argument that the GOP would pay for it with cuts in vital social services. In his day-to-day counsel to the President, Morris knew the Republicans would fall for the trap because he had spent his life in the GOP and knew the center of gravity among Republicans could not resist an invitation to shred the New Deal safety net. Check and mate.

CHAPTER FOUR

Picking Kemp

Steve Forbes would not be the nominee in 1996, but his seemingly quixotic campaign had demonstrated excitement about the idea of using a strategy of economic growth built around fundamental tax reform. Bob Dole had spent his Senate years in the budget-balancing wing of the GOP – with even Newt Gingrich once terming him "the tax collector for the welfare state." It simply was not credible that Dole could present himself to the electorate as a growth candidate who would prevent Gingrich from shredding the safety net.

A GOP *growth strategy* to overcome the public's distrust of the Republican agenda had to mean Dole would be led in the direction of Jack Kemp when looking for a running mate. It seemed so at the time, even though informed opinion was universal in saying Dole would never pick Kemp, for 20 years the leader of the GOP's growth wing. On March 15, a week after Steve Forbes dropped out of the race, it was clear that: "The biggest winner of all is Jack Kemp...In finally bolting last week, endorsing Steve Forbes *the day after* Dole swept the seven primaries of Junior Super Tuesday, Jack has established himself as the active leader of the Reaganauts, a man once again willing to throw the long ball even if it doesn't result in a score. A week ago, Jack may have been wondering if he might be offered an ambassadorship to Palookaville in a Dole administration. Today, he is vice presidential material, whether Dole likes it or not."[1]

---

1 Jude Wanniski, "Dole at a Crossroad," Polyconomics, Inc., Morristown, N.J., March 15, 1996. "Remember, the political idea being expressed a year ago was that because the GOP interpreted its 1994 mandate as a call to budget-balancing austerity, the electorate would never give the White House to the GOP if its nominee was also a root-canal austerian. Reagan Democrats would stick with Clinton if the GOP picked Bob Dole."

Picking Kemp

A mere two weeks later, it was still more apparent: "As Dole gets closer to San Diego, he will find the consensus forming around Kemp, the logical choice to unite the party and help the GOP win the blue-collar and black votes it will need to gain the White House and retain the Congress."[2]

The convoluted path Kemp traveled on the way to San Diego and the Dole ticket has been largely unreported.[3] Perhaps he could have done nothing at all between March 15 and August 7, when he got the call from Dole only a week prior to the convention. Kemp's assumption that Dole would not run the kind of growth campaign necessary to win led Jack into a series of private discussions with the Reform Party about the possibility that he might be its nominee instead of Ross Perot. I had initiated the discussions with a call to Russell Verney, the man Perot had chosen after his 1992 run to build the Reform Party into an organized national force. Verney offered repeated assurances that Perot was serious in saying that he "would build it and they would come," meaning other contenders for the party's presidential nomination. There remains today the firm conviction in the political establishment that Perot would never have permitted anyone other than himself to head the ticket in 1996, but dozens of conversations with Verney persuaded me that he and Perot would have *preferred* Kemp above all others to be their party's nominee in 1996.

If nothing else, Perot is a populist wary of Big Government and Big Business, a champion of entrepreneurial capitalism. He ran in 1992 only because he saw both George Bush and the likely Democratic candidate, Bill Clinton, as representatives of the corporate ruling class. When he decided to run, the first people he reached

---

2 Jude Wanniski, "Notes on the Revolution XXXII," Polyconomics, Inc., Morristown, N.J., March 29, 1996.

3 In the November 18 *Time* special post-election edition, Kemp suddenly appears on the ticket without a word about how he got there, only to then disappear into the mist, with scarcely a mention thereafter. That account and others helped persuade me to write this perspective.

for were people close to Kemp. Perot invited Wall Street financier Ted Forstmann to Dallas after he read a *Wall Street Journal* op-ed Forstmann had written which hit home.[4] A few days later, he invited me to Dallas after meeting with Forstmann. I spent a morning discussing politics and economics with him. In a subsequent memo, I encouraged him to bring one of Kemp's best friends, Vin Weber, in as his campaign manager, as Weber had announced he would soon be leaving Congress anyway. Perot sent his closest business friends, Mort Meyerson and Tom Luce, to meet Weber, and while he demurred, he referred them to his friend Ed Rollins. Rollins, who was to prove a disaster to the Perot campaign, accepted the job. All this made it absolutely clear that Perot felt more comfortable with Kemp and his ideas than the GOP elements associated with Big Business.

Four years later, in late March 1996, Verney flew to Washington, D.C., from his party headquarters in Dallas to meet with John Sears and me to discuss the possibility of Kemp becoming the Reform Party nominee.[5] Kemp was persuaded to drop by the evening meeting to hear what Verney had to say and was impressed enough to come by again the next morning for another discussion of Perot's intentions. Verney subsequently returned for a separate meeting with Sears, who, while skeptical that anything would come of the discussions, advised Kemp to treat them as a serious option. Sears even advised Kemp to allow his name to go out on the preferential survey that Verney had prepared, which would have automatically made Kemp eligible for the nomination, but Kemp called Verney at the last minute and withdrew his name. He realized it would appear

---

4 Theodore J. Forstmann, "Free Entrepreneurs to Fix the Economy," *The Wall Street Journal*, March 31, 1995, p. A16. The heart of the op-ed was his argument to eliminate the capital gains tax: "When capital is scarce, it is reserved for the 'sure things.' The current credit crunch simply reflects the difficulty of new enterprises in acquiring capital from the system. Capitalism must provide large rewards for large risks. Eliminating the capital-gains tax entirely will maximize the reward for risk-taking, innovation and enterprises – enabling capital to flow into long shots, because only one need win to make the entire portfolio of bets worthwhile."

5 Sears did not attend the meetings at my suite in One Washington Circle hotel, due to an illness in his immediate family that day.

in the survey with only Perot's name and that of former Colorado Governor Richard Lamm. It would be taken as a genuine signal of Kemp's willingness to bolt the GOP, or at least would be taken as an inferential slap at Dole.

Through a Sears meeting with Verney, Kemp indicated he might be willing to be the RP candidate *only if it became clear that the Dole candidacy would be dead on arrival at the San Diego convention* – and that the Reform Party would offer the nomination on a silver platter. The discussion did not seem at all incredible at the time, although Sears advised Kemp it was only an extreme longshot that he should keep alive. With Clinton leading Dole by 20 points in all the opinion polls at this time, the GOP political establishment was persuading itself that it had to assume a Dole defeat of major proportions in November. None of this talk was public, but the political grapevines had been humming on this theme as soon as it became obvious that Clinton had won the PR war with Gingrich. Obviously, a strategy had to be devised to protect Republican control of Congress. Kemp and others at the staff level were telling me at the time of an emerging consensus at the party's highest levels – Clinton would be re-elected and a strategy had to be developed to save the Congress. On a shuttle flight from DC to Newark in April, Lou Dobbs of CNN's "Moneyline" told me he had attended a GOP dinner the night before and sat at Newt Gingrich's table, and was astonished when Gingrich told the table he had to *assume* Dole would lose and that the party had to concentrate on keeping control of Congress. It was of course a prudent assumption, but the fact that Gingrich would be so open about it at a GOP gala reminds us how bleak Dole's chances seemed so soon after he'd clinched the nomination.

In her post-election book, *Whatever It Takes*, Elizabeth Drew's central theme is that Republican leaders "decided to throw Dole overboard much earlier than was realized...lest his inept campaign get in the way of their more pressing goals," but even she does not trace the idea as far back as the early spring:

The House Republicans' decision to go ahead with a separate welfare bill came during the same week as Dole's bungling on the assault weapons ban. A Republican strategist said, "The general House disgust with Dole had grown and grown – to the point where it boiled over." After holding off for a while, [RNC Chairman] Haley Barbour now championed the strategy of the House Republicans helping themselves – regardless of what the Dole people thought. Enough is enough, Barbour decided. This was not the only time that Barbour – a stumpy man with a slow Mississippi drawl and a killer mind – when faced with a choice between retaining control of the Congress and trying to save Dole, chose the Congress. Barbour would argue that these were compatible goals, but after a certain point – when it came to important decisions about allocation of resources or whose political exigencies should have supremacy – they weren't. Gingrich had held out, trying to help Dole, but in the end, in a leadership meeting on July 11th, he accepted the fact that the other House Republican leaders would insist that the House take up the [welfare] bill anyway.[6]

In his campaign review, *Behind the Oval Office*, Dick Morris cites the GOP decision to pass legislation in the summer of 1996, including the welfare bill, as a sign it had given up on Dole. If the party was serious about helping Dole, he argued, it should instead have continued to sharpen the issues between Congress and the White House: "It was this decision by [Senate Majority Leader Trent] Lott that probably won the Senate, and likely the House too, for the GOP in the '96 election. Had the Republicans remained obstinate, the voters would have rejected them decisively. But when Senator Lott assumed the majority leadership and made it clear that the deadlock was over, he sent signals to the electorate that the GOP would hereafter work to

---

6 Elizabeth Drew, *Whatever It Takes* (New York, N.Y.: Viking Penguin, 1997), p. 99.

influence legislation, not to kill it. He also showed that the Republicans had their fill of extremism by moving in the direction of the president's agenda – welfare reform, health-care portability, environmental protection, safe drinking water, and the minimum wage."[7]

Once this strategy was firmly embedded at the top of the GOP hierarchy, it became the paradigm for the national elections. There was an almost unavoidable tilt against the top of the ticket in order to optimize party strength lower in the ranks. In other words, if the electorate did not trust Dole and Gingrich together, or Clinton and the Democrats together, a Dole victory might be accompanied by the GOP loss of the House, or a Clinton victory might require the voters to return the Congress to the GOP. Indeed, when Clinton decided to sign the welfare bill instead of vetoing it, he was clearly placing his re-election above the goal of winning back control of Congress. As in a chess game, when you face an almost certain loss, there is a definite incentive to play for stalemate. In this case, the incumbents of both parties decided to play to a gentlemanly draw.

It was because Kemp was persuaded that another four more years of stalemate might not be in the national interest that he entertained the idea of running on the Reform Party ticket. Sears insisted Kemp could not appear to be angling for the nomination, but would have to be drafted. Verney offered assurances that Kemp could bring his own agenda. Only two conditions were laid down by Perot, said Verney, one being that no special-interest money be accepted in furtherance of the campaign and that there would be no personal attacks on the other candidates. On June 18, *The Wall Street Journal* carried an essay by Kemp that laid out an economic agenda which could be adopted by any of the three political parties.[8] To a degree, the essay was crafted to find out if it would be acceptable to Perot. Kemp was essentially signaling that if he were President,

---

7 Dick Morris, *Behind the Oval Office* (New York, N.Y.: Random House, 1997), p. 297.

the very first thing he would do would be to sign executive orders indexing capital gains retroactively and stabilizing the price of gold. If the agenda were not acceptable to Perot, that would be the end of any discussions. Word immediately came back from Verney that Perot had no problem with it, although he raised a few technical questions involving Kemp's position on fixing the price of gold by executive order to dramatically lower interest rates. Kemp was practically assured the Reform Party nomination if he signaled his willingness to accept it by allowing it to appear on the nominating survey. But a key deadline passed with Kemp unwilling to test the waters further, believing such a signal would be considered a stab in Dole's back, as it would have.

It was at this point that Kemp's flirtation with the Reform Party became known publicly. *The New York Times* carried a story by Ernest Tollerson which reported Kemp's refusal to allow his name to be added to the party's preferential survey.[9] Trent Lott warned Kemp that Perot was just using him to elevate himself, and would control the outcome of the nomination process. Verney insisted that the people eligible to vote in the nomination process were not hard-core Perotistas and that if Kemp put his name forward, he was practically assured the nomination. At that point, Perot had not even signaled his interest in being on top of the ticket, awaiting the outcome of the discussions. The tiny number of people who subsequently sent in their nominating ballots confirmed what Verney had been saying: Kemp would easily have gotten the nomination if he had even given his passive assent in allowing his name to appear on the preferential survey.

The background of Kemp's momentary contact with the Reform Party surfaced in a July 8 column by Robert Novak, which appeared in *The Washington Post.* Novak wrote about the attempts to promote

---

8 Jack Kemp, "A Bipartisan Economic Agenda," *The Wall Street Journal,* June 18, 1996, p. A22.

9 Ernest Tollerson, "Perot's Party Plans to Mail Survey to Select a Nominee," *The New York Times,* July 3, 1996, p. A11.

a draft-Kemp movement in the Reform Party. He made it clear that the Reform Party would love to have Kemp enter the process, but that Kemp had thus far spurned the overtures. He also made it clear the idea was not moribund. More importantly, Novak reported that "[John] Sears, conceded even by critics to have one of the keenest minds in American politics, told me he believes Kemp could win. The basis for that remarkable conclusion is something nearly everybody agrees on: Clinton's double-digit lead over Dole is deceptive. Internals of polls show Americans are dissatisfied with both candidates and are looking for something else."[10]

It was, though, even more complex. "Neither Sears, who was Reagan's campaign manager in 1976 and 1980, and Mark Nuttle, who was Pat Robertson's campaign manager in 1988, believe that Dole can win a three-way race if Perot or [Richard] Lamm head the Reform ticket. They also surmise that many Republicans who would normally vote the top of the ticket and down the line would chill out and stay home, opening the possibility of broader Democratic victories. With Kemp at the top, the reverse would occur, with voters not only coming out to vote for the Reform Party candidate, but also casting their votes for GOP candidates who have won the endorsement of the Reform Party...[Dole's] only salvation could be a Dole-Kemp ticket that is driven by Kemp's agenda, brought about by these pressures."[11] Yet, the race remained a race as long as the policy gridlock in the government "is the result of the tax system and campaign finance, which perpetuates the status quo. Unless the gridlock is broken by an outside force, we almost certainly will stumble along into the next century. It is against this hard assumption that I can even imagine a quixotic scenario that brings Perot himself to the Oval Office, with a running mate and a Cabinet capable of doing the job."[12]

---

10 Robert Novak, "A Kemp Campaign? Negative," *The Washington Post,* July 8, 1996, p. A15.

11 Jude Wanniski, "Clinton vs. Dole vs. Perot," Polyconomics, Inc., Morristown, N.J., July 10, 1996.

Behind this observation was the lingering possibility that Kemp might be persuaded to be Perot's running mate, after the GOP convention in San Diego concluded with a Dole-Whomever ticket that would invite universal opinion of doom. On a trip to Washington in June, I met with Trent Lott in his Senate office and advised him I was developing this option for Kemp and that Jack was allowing me to keep the option in play. Lott told me that we should instead be working to get Kemp on the ticket with Dole, to which I readily agreed, but pointed out that he and I were the only two people in the universe who thought that was a possibility.

Lott, a courtly Mississippian with a gift for getting people to work together, came to Congress in 1973 as a House member, when Kemp was taking the lead in promoting the supply-side revolution. He was recruited by Kemp as one of four lieutenants who brought the ideas to realization. The other three were Newt Gingrich of Georgia, Connie Mack of Florida, and Vin Weber of Minnesota. Of the four, Lott was most senior, becoming Minority Whip in the House before his election to the Senate in 1988. In the 20 years since this team of five extraordinary men was first taking shape, they held together as friends, the amigos, as they called themselves, at frequent dinners that were first hosted by Kemp at his home in Bethesda, Maryland. The purpose was to keep the team together around the original growth agenda, even though each of the amigos had developed far beyond the junior status they had when Kemp first assembled the team. In July of this year, the power of the team was phenomenal. Lott was Senate Majority Leader; Gingrich the Speaker of the House; Mack the chairman of the Joint Economic Committee in the Senate; Weber the co-chairman of the Dole for President committee. Kemp had no formal position, a private citizen who had only recently irritated the party establishment by endorsing Steve Forbes when it was clear Forbes had lost his own run at power. Indeed, Kemp's endorsement of Forbes had so infuriated Gingrich, who had

---

12 Ibid.

been his lieutenant a dozen years ago, that he publicly denounced Kemp and let it be known they were no longer on speaking terms.

The two did not speak for four months, until the evening of Friday, July 19, when the five amigos arranged to have their first meeting since Kemp's endorsement of Forbes. At the meeting, Gingrich berated Kemp for his continued flirtation with Perot and the Reform Party. Kemp insisted that there were some things more important than the party, and the growth idea he represented was one of them. Growth is what had bound them together, yet Gingrich had not mentioned the word for six months, said Kemp, as the argument heated up. The mild-mannered Senator Mack of Florida finally protested and said if this was what their group had come to, he was leaving, and it would be the last he would attend. Kemp quickly apologized for raising his voice. Gingrich said no, he should apologize, and that Kemp was right. He had allowed the growth issue to get away from him, but it should be brought back on track for the campaign ahead of all those in the party. They asked Kemp to supervise a day of discussion the following week, a one-day summit of GOP leaders, to put taxes and growth back into focus. The meeting of amigos ended warmly, the air having been cleared.

The one-day economic summit held the following Tuesday, July 23, not only brought the growth agenda back to the top of the GOP agenda, it also brought Kemp into the good graces of the party. It was at this point that the idea of Kemp joining Dole on the ticket truly became feasible and took root. The only other serious last-minute contender was Connie Mack, who had never crossed swords with Dole as Kemp had over the years. (A year later, looking back on his decision, Dole suggested to an interviewer that Mack might have been the better choice, but then retracted the thought and said he had no regrets, that Kemp had worked as hard as he, Dole, had.) The summit also produced a consensus among the senior party leaders to put supply-side tax cuts into the mix for the national campaign. The consensus included those who had in the past been identified with fiscal austerity and balanced budgets, including Senate Budget Chairman Pete Domenici. The co-chairman of the Dole campaign, Donald Rumsfeld, described in the press as a deficit hawk, also attended and embraced a commitment to tax cuts that would have positive revenue effects. There was sufficient significance in the event to predict an end to the bearish sentiment on Wall Street[13] and, in fact, the market hit its low for the period the day of the summit: "The darkest days on the NASDAQ may now be behind us...[the Dole tax plan] even if Bill Clinton wins re-election, would lead to a voter turnout that would produce a Republican Congress clearly committed to putting the economic horse ahead of the downsizing cart."[14]

At the time, there was no specific "Dole tax plan," only a consensus to present one. As much as the Old Guard hated the idea of tax cuts with the budget in deficit, it knew the national ticket could not go to the voters without *something* reminiscent of the Gipper. A group of academic economists had been meeting since May 8 on Capitol Hill to devise a plan. It had been initiated by Senator Domenici, a deficit hawk and one of Dole's closest friends in the Senate. He had asked Michael Boskin, chairman of President Bush's Council of Economic Advisers, to pull together a team. Boskin wisely realized he was too closely identified with Bush and would raise the hackles of all those who blamed the loss of the White House on the 1990 tax increase. Boskin recommended John Taylor, a fellow Stanford economist who had been his No. 2 man at the CEA, to chair the task force.

As the sessions evolved, one alternative involved rolling back the Bush tax increase of 1990 and the Clinton tax increase of 1993. This was a plan advocated by Kemp and Steve Forbes, a plan urged by a team of supply-side economists who had worked in the Reagan

---

13 Jude Wanniski, "To the Tax Issue," Polyconomics, Inc., Morristown, N.J., July 25, 1996. Just three days earlier, on July 22, Elaine Garzarelli, one of the most bullish analysts on Wall Street, had thrown in the towel and called for a major selloff.
14 Ibid.

Treasury department. Forbes, who attended some of the meetings, was alone in carrying the ball on its behalf. The group that had designed it never appeared to argue its case, apparently because nobody thought to ask them. They had persuaded Kemp and Forbes to support the rollback plan and had argued vehemently against a second plan first suggested in a *Washington Times* column by Bruce Bartlett, who had worked in the Bush Treasury department. He had recommended a 15 percent across-the-board tax cut that would make Dole seem Reaganesque, replicating Reagan's 1980 promise to cut income tax rates by a third.[15] Taylor, a competent, mild-mannered professor with no real political sense, had been briefed by Kemp's people on the political flaws in the 15 percent plan, but there is no record that he conveyed these warnings to the task force, and Taylor meekly acquiesced to the political arguments of behalf of the 15 percent plan that came to dominate the meetings. Taylor understood the plan was not only for the benefit of Dole, but to give GOP members of Congress something *simple* enough to grasp and campaign on.

As the idea evolved into a larger plan, it came to include an unindexed halving of the capital gains tax, and a $500 per child tax credit. Including the $500 kiddie credit, as we had been calling it, was the clearest evidence the plan had far less to do with supply-side economics than with political calculations which assumed the gullibility of the voting public. A 15 percent across-the-board income-tax cut could be defended on economic grounds, but only barely. Because the President and the Democratic Congress had raised the income tax to 39 from 31 percent in the 1993 budget, a 15 percent cut in the top rate would only bring it to 33 percent, still five points higher than the 28 percent rate Reagan had engineered in the 1986 tax reform. The halving of the capital gains tax could be easily defended, but because the Dole economic experts had close to zero

---

15 Bruce Bartlett, "Evidence of the Tax Bite that Keeps Growing," *The Washington Times*, April 29, 1996, p. 7A.

expertise in the technicalities of the federal tax codes, they did not realize they should have offered a 50 percent exclusion on capital gains income instead of a lowering of the rate itself. This is because Democrats in earlier years had put into the tax code an "Alternative Minimum Tax" provision that had been designed to prevent the avoidance of all tax by the rich through sheltered investments. Excluding 50 percent of capgains would result in a genuine reduction for all taxpayers reporting gains; a 50 percent rate cut would continue to subject the same gain to a second tax under the AMT provision. As a result of this and other technical errors made by the Dole team, the plan was not only an indefensible embarrassment, but also would cause a tax increase to 9 million middle-class taxpayers if it were enacted as proposed.[16]

The Kemp team's argument was that the Treasury estimate of the cost of the 15 percent plan, at $548 billion over six years, would be 60 percent more expensive than the rollback plan. This is because the Democrats in 1993 had designed the tax increase to hit higher reported incomes, which only a small proportion of the total workforce enjoyed. Revenues "lost" as a result of a rollback to 31 percent would be relatively small and could be justified more easily on political as well as economic grounds. The Kemp team argued the 15 percent plan would enable the Democrats to continue arguing that the Dole tax cuts would have to be paid for by cutting Medicare and other social programs. Until the last minute, the press was indicating the rollback plan was favored. On August 5, the campaign announced the 15 percent plan. The Kemp team was shocked and demoralized by the decision. Within hours of the announcement Kemp believed Dole had just thrown away his last chance at winning the election. I wrote at the time:

---

16 President Clinton's Treasury team, which ran the numbers, quickly made this discovery, and in the closing weeks of the campaign, the President frequently mentioned the fact that the Dole plan would cause a tax increase to 9 million Americans.

Dole...will run into the buzz saw that Newt Gingrich encountered on Medicare and Medicaid. It's hard to imagine him
defending the plan against the attacks that will be made by
the Clinton campaign and Democrats in general. It would
have been easier to argue simply that President Bush made
a mistake in 1990 and President Clinton made one in 1993.
To them, he would not have had to put on a supply-side hat
or pose as the Gipper. He could simply have argued that the
tax increases in both instances did not work as planned,
because the higher rates imposed on the 'rich' did not produce the revenues they were supposed to produce...The
argument that the rollback would benefit the 'rich' could
be taken care of by spending some of the 'savings' in the
rollback option to permit deductibility of payroll taxes and
an increase in the personal exemption. This would have
enabled Dole to comfortably defend the distributional
effects on rich versus poor. In the plan he has chosen, only
1 percent or so of the benefits go to the bottom 20 percent
of the income classes. We have no idea why Dole feels more
comfortable with the approach he has taken, but believe
this will not last very long. It is amazing that Dole continues to come down on the wrong side of every issue he
encounters. It is especially puzzling that in choosing to suit
up as a 'supply-sider' he would reject the ideas and arguments of the two leading supply-siders in the GOP, Kemp
and Forbes.[17]

The following day, *The New York Times* published "Hoover's
Heirs," which criticized the Concord Coalition, a balance-the-
budget lobby group, for taking the position "that the economy can't
grow much faster than it currently is," although saying "the coalition is on solid ground to oppose the kind of large tax cut Mr. Dole

---

17 Jude Wanniski, "Problems With the Dole Tax Plan," Polyconomics, Inc.,
Morristown, N.J., August 5, 1996.

proposes." The opening paragraphs summarize the issues at that moment:

> In a recent interview, President Clinton shared with us his dismay that nobody really knows how fast the economy can grow without inflation.
>
> This is the biggest issue facing the President as well as Bob Dole and Ross Perot's Reform Party. If the economy can grow at 5 percent a year for several years without inflation, as most supply-siders believe, the impossible problems of future financing for Medicare and Social Security would dissolve. But if our growth rate cannot exceed 3 percent, even for a short time, these programs will bankrupt the nation.
>
> The $548 billion tax cut that Mr. Dole presented yesterday points in the right direction but is very expensive for what it would yield in added economic growth. The only real kick to the economy is the proposed $13 billion cut in the capital gains tax. The rest would be nice to have but would do little to encourage sustained growth.[18]

In other words, the contemporaneous record shows that there was supply-side unhappiness with the Dole tax plan, and those historians interested in where the 15 percent plan came from would find abundant evidence that *it was a defeat for Kemp*. The defeat was so startling that those of us who still believed there was a chance Kemp would be picked by Dole as his running mate were now sure we were wrong. It was taken as a slap in the face by Kemp and his followers. As so often happens in political campaigns, Dole probably never knew about Kemp's opposition to the 15 percent plan. John Taylor subsequently said he did not know of Kemp's opposition until *after* the decision had been made. He told me later that he thought both plans were economically sound, but the political people

---

18 Jude Wanniski, "Hoover's Heirs," *The New York Times*, August 6, 1996, p. A17.

Picking Kemp

– Scott Reed's team – believed the 15 percent plan would be an easier one on which to campaign. The warnings of the Kemp team to the contrary were clearly not being heard or understood. This oversight was to be one of the greatest burdens upon the campaign to the very end. The Clinton team characterized it as "a risky scheme that would blow a hole in the budget," a phrase repeated six times by Vice President Gore in his debate with Kemp. Ross Perot characterized it as a candy giveaway. In the last week of the campaign, Representative John Kasich [R-OH], chairman of the House Budget Committee, needled the Dole campaign for having tried to sell it as candy for the voters, instead of as part of a plan to get the whole country on the move.

Still, both Kemp and Forbes that night appeared on "Larry King Live" to promote the tax plan they or their advisors had fought.[19] Kemp was so sure he had been cut out that he indicated he might not bother going to the San Diego convention the following week, changing his mind when his wife Joanne pointed out that they would cause comment in being absent, and should at least put in an appearance. Kemp's good soldiering on the Monday TV program, though, may have helped the campaign's decision to move seriously toward him as Dole's running mate. It was the following day that he was called and invited to meet with Dole at his Watergate apartment. It was the day after, August 7, when a story appeared in *The New York Times* that Kemp had been added to the list of possible running mates. I called Kemp that morning at home, told him his name was in play, and I believed it meant they would offer him the slot. He had already met with Dole, but did not indicate to me that he had. I practically begged him to contact John Sears, to get his

---

19 The advisors included Gary and Aldonna Robbins of Fiscal Associates, Steve Entin, a partner with Norman Ture Associates, and Lawrence Hunter, chief economist at Empower America and former chief economist of the U.S. Chamber of Commerce. The Robbinses and Entin worked in the Reagan Treasury tax division. Hunter also served as chief minority counsel to the Joint Economic Committee of Congress.

advice and ask him to represent his interests *before* he accepted the Dole offer. Given the way we had been trampled in the decision on taxes, I was fearful Kemp would not be brought in as the partner *with the ideas*, but as an appendage to follow orders. Hardly excited by the prospect, I urged Jack to use Sears to nail down a "prenuptial agreement."

Early on Friday the 9th, after reading the papers at 7 a.m., I faxed a note from home to Russ Verney, Perot's man, who still held out hope that Kemp would run with Perot on the Reform Party ticket. Of course, that was now by the boards:

> It certainly is beginning to look like this is it. I didn't have the slightest inkling that this was going to happen, although I have been saying for months it is the only possible way for Dole to unite the GOP. I'm almost sure Elizabeth Dole has been the instigator. I've been saying for the last few weeks that she has been saying nice things about Jack. I'm told that the decision is being made by the Doles and Scott Reed, which pretty much says it all. I haven't talked to Jack since he met with Dole, but I imagine he is setting some conditions of his own if he is to join a campaign that seems so hopeless at this point. If Jack were to get enough control over the conduct of the campaign, accentuating the positive, I think Dole-Kemp would definitely cut into the Clinton lead. It might also draw away what interest there is in Ross. My guess that in this scenario there would be serious efforts to have Ross and the Reform Party throw its support at the presidential level to Dole-Kemp...I think Ross would have to seriously consider this, knowing he would put Dole in the White House.

That day, Kemp accepted the offer and prepared to fly to Kansas, where the announcement would be made the following afternoon. Sears was contacted at his home in Washington and asked to fly ahead to San Diego to begin the process of integrating with the Dole team.[20] Sears agreed, said he would leave immediately, and called to ask me to join him in San Diego to help with Kemp's acceptance speech. On Sunday when I arrived, he had been there 24 hours and had a first assessment of the situation after meeting with the Dole team. *There is no strategy on how to win the election,* he said. *They only know they are going to spend a lot of money on TV spots.*

The convention was not an encouraging experience. It quickly became obvious that the Dole campaign, which had been evolving from a standing start 18 months earlier, had a definite momentum even if it did not have a strategy. Nobody was really in charge, except, ultimately, the candidate. "It," the campaign, was not simply a group of people, but an organism that had taken its shape around the needs of the candidate and his personality and the political forces that impinged upon it from day to day. It slowed just enough to pick up Kemp as a passenger, but there was never a time thereafter when it showed much interest in his ideas on how the election might be won. It seemed driven by an internal impulse for survival rather than success, a wary outlook on anything that might cause a mistake to be made. If the party is geared for its own self-preservation, a campaign is geared for self-preservation plus. Risk-taking is actively discouraged, rather than entertained. Clearly, Kemp and his people had to be housebroken. I still had a faint hope that Sears would rouse himself to the possibility that a Dole-Kemp ticket could win and refuse to be tamed. If he asserted himself, he would be able to muscle the rest of the team, several of whom were his protégés. This hope was soon dashed. Sears simply refused to believe the voters would choose Dole over Clinton and decided to go along just for the ride, with the sole purpose of helping Kemp survive the debacle he anticipated and live to fight another day.

---

20 After the campaign, Sears told me it was never realistic to think of the Dole-Kemp ticket as being a marriage between the two men. Kemp, he said, was more the "kept woman," which is always the way a presidential campaign tends to treat the vice presidential nominee.

It was not easy to disagree. Any disinterested observer would have noticed the day before Kemp's name surfaced that the Dole campaign was moribund, the Republican Party gloomily hanging crepe around the convention city. A day later, the same observer would have noticed an explosion of life in San Diego and enthusiasm for the ticket in the news media. *This ticket could win!* Why, then, would Sears arrive and find that the Dole people had already hired professional speechwriters to draft Kemp's acceptance speech? The speech was dreadful, a string of cliches that caricatured Kemp as a football playing tax cutter. This was hardly the fault of the writers, who were competent and talented, but who scarcely knew Kemp and had not talked to him before sitting down to write. Worse, they were instructed to draft the speech in conformance with the findings of Tony Fabrizio, the campaign pollster. At the first speech meeting with Kemp, the writers, and representatives of the Dole team, Sears lost no time in pronouncing the speech draft "hackneyed." The word reverberated through the room as if a stick of dynamite had gone off. The writers were in the room and so were the Dole people who approved the words. It was one of the last real blows struck by Sears, who soon thereafter saw there was no point in fighting and went with the flow for the duration of the campaign. As for the Kemp speech, there were several marathon drafting sessions that finally resulted in the version delivered in the convention hall. Yet it was made plain throughout the process that Kemp had to bend to Fabrizio's polls.[21] There was a definite command structure that relegated Kemp to the role of a spear carrier.

The naive expectation that this would be a partnership between Dole and Kemp ended with the realization that Kemp's people would not be shown an advance copy of Dole's acceptance speech. Writers had been working on Dole's speech for *months* and yet it was apparently no closer to completion as the convention opened than was the first hackneyed draft prepared for Kemp on August 11, the day before the convention officially began. It was clear to me when I sat in the hall and heard Dole deliver it why his campaign wanted no advance critique from Kemp or his people. With Dole speaking to the biggest national audience he would have in the entire campaign, he delivered a *screech* designed as pure red meat for the right wing faction in the party. There were whiffs of inclusiveness toward minorities here and there, with Dole inviting bigots to leave the hall in the most constructive moment of his speech. But if he was trying to reassure the electorate that it could trust him to restrain the dark impulses in the GOP that the Democrats were making the primary bogeymen of the campaign, the speech helped not one bit.

The most vivid image was of Dole snarling through his lines on crime: "We are a nation paralyzed by crime, and it is time to end that in America. And to do so, to do so, I mean to attack the root causes of crime – criminals, criminals, violent criminals. And as our many and voracious criminals go to bed tonight, at, say, six in the morning, they had better pray that I lose the election. Because if I win, the lives of violent criminals are going to be hell." To the Dole people, this was a line obviously designed to close the gender gap, as if women wanted lawbreakers boiled in oil. It would have exactly the opposite effect, underscoring Dole's image as a vengeful and wrathful man, a Gingrich comrade-in-arms.

There was also Dole's shrill pledge to break the back of the teachers union, in a passage that surely scared the daylights out of any kindergarten kids who happened to be watching: to "the teachers unions I say, when I am President, I will disregard your political power, for the sake of the parents, the children, the schools and the nation." In this segment of the speech, which lasted several minutes, he said he would get the nation's governors to deny parole to violent

---

21 I had either drafted or worked on the drafts of Kemp's GOP convention speeches in 1976, 1980, 1984, 1988 and 1992. In San Diego, I was not permitted in the room with the writers when they were working. The few suggestions I made on paper were summarily rejected without comment.

criminals, that he would only appoint judges who would be "intolerant of outrage." He said he was "prepared to risk more political capital in defense of domestic tranquility than any President you have ever known." In foreign affairs, Dole vowed that on "my first day in office I will put America on a course that will end our vulnerability to missile attack," by building up America's military might, as if the Third World War were right around the corner.[22] I was shocked and frankly sickened by the coarseness and anger in the speech. Since I'd met him in 1969, I'd gotten to know Dole almost as well as I knew any politician and I knew that, were he a state governor, he would be a pushover for a clemency appeal on behalf of a prisoner who did not deserve to have the key thrown away. Dole had evidently decided to let his handlers run the campaign, on the grounds that whenever he ran it, he lost, and was told he was a bad campaign manager.

At the worst moments in the Dole acceptance speech, my wife Patricia, a registered Democrat who had reluctantly voted for Bush in 1988 and 1992, turned to me and said, "I don't belong here." As we left the hall with our sourpusses, we ran into Representative Jennifer Dunn [R-WA], who asked us why we seemed so unhappy. I told her about the way I'd hoped he would speak to the nation in his acceptance speech, but instead threw red meat to the right wing. She made a comment that seemed to connect with our concerns, but then gave Dole the last word: "Maybe he felt he had to solidify his base."

---

22   Richard L. Berke, "Dole, the Most Optimistic Man in America, Vows to Return to America's Enduring Values," *The New York Times*, August 16, 1996, p. A1.

CHAPTER FIVE

"We Have a Fabrizio Problem"

*T*he art of polling is very much like the weather; everyone complains about it but no one can figure out what to do about it. Polling is ubiquitous and even sometimes useful, but more frequently it can be misused to prove a particular point. It is dangerous to build a campaign around polls, as a slight variation in the phrasing of a question can produce dramatically different results, and the candidate runs the risk of appearing either to toady to the electorate or to be weak and ineffective in the vision area.

Immediately after Dole's speech to the convention, which was in and of itself a bow to the polling power of his staff, Ted Forstmann, the Wall Street financier and Kemp ally who had co-founded Empower America, was hosting a dinner for about 20 friends at a restaurant near the convention hall. Kemp did not attend the hastily arranged dinner, but this was clearly his gang. Pete Rozelle, the former NFL commissioner and one of Kemp's oldest friends, sat at one end of the table, clearly struggling with a brain cancer that would take his life a few months later. Also there were the two co-chairman of the Dole campaign, Donald Rumsfeld and Vin Weber. You would assume these were Dole people, but for practical purposes they were, and remain, closer to Kemp than to Dole. They were both on the board of directors of Kemp's Empower America before Dole chose them to nominally head his campaign team. "Co-chairman" slots were powerless positions, with no authority to hire or fire, to schedule or to channel resources to campaign advertising. They were guaranteed seats at the daily meetings which chewed incessantly over the polls and grumbled about the unfairness of the press corps, but they had no real power to alter the direction of the campaign.

"We Have a Fabrizio Problem"

Rumsfeld had been President Gerald Ford's White House Chief of Staff and later Secretary of Defense. He and I had been casual political friends from his days in the House of Representatives when I was columnizing for *The National Observer*. I actually hosted an *Observer* dinner in 1969 at the *old* Willard Hotel for Rumsfeld when he was Nixon's director of the Office of Economic Opportunity, and his general factotum was a young man named Richard Cheney. In 1978, when I founded Polyconomics, Rumsfeld, who was CEO of the Illinois pharmaceutical company, G.D. Searle, became my second paying client after Chrysler Corporation.

At the 1980 convention in Detroit that nominated Reagan, I persuaded a friend at *The Detroit News* to write a lead editorial promoting Rumsfeld as a potential Reagan running mate. Rumsfeld did not make the ticket, but we remained friends. After he left Searle, Forstmann hired him to run General Instruments and asked him to serve on Empower America at its founding in late 1992. A year or two older than Kemp, Rumsfeld was always a better political manager than a politician, with the kind of edge that enabled him to succeed at G.D. Searle by cutting through deadwood the way Al "Chainsaw" Phillips would do a generation later in corporate America. Still, he was clearly in the GOP's "growth wing," and had been instrumental in persuading President Ford to drop his plans for a tax increase in 1974 and promote a tax cut. Ford fumbled by backing a tax rebate instead of a cut. Still, I counted Rumsfeld as one of the few allies I had inside the Dole campaign. I'd also been close to Weber, the other co-chairman, 20 years younger than Rumsfeld but a Washington player for almost 20 years.

At this point, as far ahead as Clinton was in the polls, and as bad a candidate Dole would be as evidenced by his dreadful acceptance speech, the pro-growth forces might still have had enough friends inside the campaign to maybe eke out a win. It was, I must admit, pretty gloomy at the Forstmann celebration dinner. Patricia and I were the first to arrive, given our unhappiness with the Dole speech and my reporter's sense of the quickest way to the exit. Minutes later Weber arrived with Jim Pinkerton, a 7-foot tall GOP policy wonk who had originally come to Washington in 1981 with Ronald Reagan and is now a columnist for *Newsday*. Neither Weber nor Pinkerton were smiling, and they did not wait to ask my opinion on what I thought of the evening in the convention hall. Weber immediately announced that he thought the Dole speech terrible for the same reason Patricia said she did not even belong in the convention hall, that she was not part of the constituency Dole sought to represent. The other guests filtering in to the dinner were cheerful enough, including Forstmann and Rumsfeld, but none of them had Weber's political nose for what it would take to get blue-collar Reaganauts and women back into the GOP column.

Both Weber and Pinkerton opined that Dole's hardline acceptance speech would overwhelm any positive effect Kemp's earlier address had made on the vast television audience that watched both men that night. All the glitz and expense of the convention extravaganza meant nothing next to the candidate's acceptance speech! As he thought about it, Weber looked at me with dark visage and confided: *"We have a Fabrizio problem."* John Sears had already indicated as much when he told me that the speech written for Kemp had been done to the campaign pollster's specifications. *In the absence of a candidate with a strategy or a candidate with a strategist, the organism of the campaign would be driven by the pollster,* Tony Fabrizio. I'd never met the man and still have not, but it would not matter. No matter how good a pollster is in polling, the individual is patently not competent to be President of the United States – a job that requires a lifetime of planning, not polling. When Weber said "We have a Fabrizio problem," it meant to me that the pollster was running for President and had massively inordinate power in the campaign. We could never solve the problem. In the last stages of the campaign, instead of snarling the line "criminals, criminals, criminals," Dole reached to the bottom of the pollster's barrel to declaim against Clinton and Gore, "Liberals! Liberals! Liberals!"

Vin Weber knew the Dole tirade against the teachers and his snarling promise to punish the criminals was going in the wrong direction if Dole was going to seem kinder and gentler than Newt. After this "co-chairman" vented his spleen about the Dole speech, which he had not seen in advance, I broke the bad news to him that there was more than a Fabrizio problem: Dole's 15 percent tax-cut plan, which had been sprung on everyone only 10 days earlier, was *technically flawed* and would be difficult to defend. *It had to be changed.* You cannot ask the national electorate for a mandate that is fundamentally flawed. As individuals they may be taken in, but as a political market, they will see the flaw and understand its backers are flawed as well. Weber knew me well enough to know I would not bring up a trivial matter, and when I talked of a deep flaw, he was all ears. Practically the whole world believed by now that Dole had chosen the 15 percent tax cut at the same time he had chosen Jack as his running mate, and that Jack was a prime mover behind the 15 percent cut instead of someone who had fought it.

I had to leave the dinner before coffee was served because the host, Ted Forstmann, who had flown to San Diego earlier in the day from New York on his Gulfstream IV (he is the chairman of Gulfstream Corp.), had offered to fly Patricia and me back with him. (He had given Patricia a ride to San Diego that morning.) The airport gave him a specific time for takeoff or he would have to wait until morning. In the few minutes I had, I sat next to Rumsfeld and told him about the serious flaw in the 15 percent tax cut. The way the Dole team had designed the plan, it would raise taxes on many millions of Americans, those most likely to support Dole. Its economic effects would be trivial, at best. At first, Rumsfeld was clearly irked at me for springing this on him, asking why I was so cocksure about my opinion when so many topflight economists had signed off on it. *Are you always right and everyone else wrong?*, he asked. I quickly explained that I had known nothing about the flaws because I am not a technical expert. My warning was based on the findings of the technical experts Kemp had used, including Larry Hunter, the chief economist of Empower America and former chief economist of the U.S. Chamber of Commerce. Rumsfeld was so flustered I could see I'd struck a nerve, later finding that he sided with the flawed 15 percent tax-cut idea instead of the rollback plan the supply-side tax experts had recommended.

As I left the restaurant, I found Weber and Rumsfeld huddled at a cocktail table outside our private dining room. I pulled up a chair to repeat my concerns and recommended they prepare a scenario in which the 15 percent tax plan would be downplayed in the campaign ahead and greater emphasis placed on a fundamental reform of the entire federal tax code. Rumsfeld, irked by my alarms, by now had cooled off. He asked me who was the best of the four economic technicians I had earlier mentioned – who should be consulted. Gary Robbins, I instantly responded, a man who had been a primary tax economist in the Reagan Treasury department with his wife Aldonna, who had worked in the Carter Treasury Department. Gary Robbins, I told him, has been the technician House Majority Leader Dick Armey had been using to vet his flat-tax proposals, I explained, and there is none better. Rumsfeld said he had never heard of him. Weber, sitting there with us, assured Rumsfeld that he knew Robbins and that he was first rate. This seemed to placate Rumsfeld. As I left, I thought perhaps we could make the necessary repairs.

It would never happen. The campaign had been put in the hands of Fabrizio's polls and nobody was going to argue with the polls.

Unfortunately, the only chance to amend the tax plan came in these first days after the GOP convention, when the press corps was still open to the idea that a change of emphasis could be attributed to Kemp's addition of expertise to the ticket. This is how I had made the argument to the co-chairmen, Rumsfeld and Weber. The next I heard, weeks later, was that the Taylor panel of economists had met, not with Gary Robbins, but with Larry Hunter of Empower America. After the meeting, Hunter called to tell me that his arguments against the plan had been drowned out by those who had designed it, along with the political people who said it was too late to shift gears without seeming to create more political problems than could be solved. *There then was no turning back.* From that point on the Dole campaign was burdened with the "risky scheme that would blow a hole in the deficit," as Vice President Al Gore intoned six times in his debate with Kemp in October. The $558 billion cost of the "risky scheme," twice the amount of the Gingrich tax cut in his Contract With America, was a *predictable* millstone around the Dole campaign from first day to last. The warning I had given Rumsfeld and Weber at the dinner went for naught. And Gary Robbins was never contacted. How many people knew in the course of the Dole-Kemp campaign that the central plank on taxes had been designed not by the Kemp people, but by the Bush people?

In his stump speeches, Kemp scarcely referred to the 15 percent tax cut, mentioning it only as a transition to the fundamental tax reform that his Tax Commission had recommended and which Dole and Gingrich had blessed. The damage had been done, though, as Kemp donned his old No. 15 football jersey from the San Diego Chargers for a photo op with Bob Dole the day after the convention nominated them. This was yet another example of the Dole media people believing that it did not matter what it took to get a picture in the public's collective visage; it should be done. The political media experts, with few exceptions, view the electorate as a mass that is crying out to be manipulated. I fired off a memo to Jack begging him to fight off any more ridiculous photo-ops with his football uniform, and thankfully there were none thereafter. (I'm sure before the end of the campaign, the Dole media people would have had me boiled in oil if they could have gotten away with it.) The Dole speechwriting team thenceforth fed "the Bobster," as GOP insiders were derisively calling him, a steady diet of the 15 percent tax cut and the $500 kiddie credit to "put more money into people's pockets."[1]

The nonsensical 15 percent tax cut, which was really a giant give-away to middle-class families with children, immediately went into the production of TV spots by the media team. The Dole television spots focused on what Ross Perot correctly called the "candy" that Dole was giving away to the voters at the expense of the budget needs. At least 80 percent of the Dole tax-cut plan would be worse than worthless, but counter-productive. The Clinton advertising and that of the Democratic Party never let the voters forget that this "candy" would have to be paid for – out of Medicare and entitlements. When the Dole campaign found the tax spots were not helping close the gap with Clinton, they pulled them off and began running against the President's character. Their favorite spot reminded voters that the President once smoked pot and didn't inhale and later told kids he would try to inhale if he did it again.

If there was going to be a serious effort to close the gap with Clinton, which was largely a gender gap, at some point the Dole media team would have to understand why the gap existed. It should have been obvious that the gap existed because those American women who were having the hardest time making ends meet were also those who were most frightened by Newt Gingrich. The President's campaign practically announced that he would use this as a lynchpin of his election strategy. The issue was economic, not cultural. Instead, the Dole campaign made the mistaken assumption that the generic "woman" was a "soccer mom" who wanted their

---

1 The phrase was one Kemp would never use and is anathema to supply-siders, who would only lower those tax rates believed to be counterproductive, i.e, producing less revenue at the higher rate because of dampening effects on economic activity. Late in the campaign, Representative John Kasich [R-OH], chairman of the House Budget Committee, criticized the Dole campaign for the way it presented the tax cut and he was quickly criticized by the Dole people for sounding a dissenting note.

"We Have a Fabrizio Problem"

President to spend his time inveighing against the use of drugs. As a result, tens of millions of dollars were squandered. The money was not only wasted. The media campaign was *reinforcing* the concern of single women and unmarried mothers – that Dole was another Gingrich, another Old Testament God of Wrath and Retribution who was ready to remove the social safety net at a moment's notice. Better to stick with New Testament Bill Clinton, who forgives sinners, being one himself.

CHAPTER SIX

Clinton and Character

T he issue of the President's fitness for office had been central to the 1992 campaign. The voters then decided upon him over President Bush or Ross Perot, even though there were serious questions President Clinton faced on the issue of character. The voters obviously were willing to put these concerns aside, seeing in him assets that overcame the liabilities. In 1996, Republican opinion leaders, especially those in the print and broadcast media, never tired of nudging their candidates in the direction of the character issue. *The Wall Street Journal* editorial page was in the forefront, persuaded in the previous four years that Bill Clinton was unfit to be President. He was, said the *Journal,* an "existentialist," who did not live by principle, but in an amoral moment-to-moment existence that played solely to his idea of power. The conservative and Christian right, two distinct factions in the party which did not always see eye to eye, came together in that year in pushing character ahead of bread-and-butter issues. On June 4, after Dole's nomination was secure, but before he revealed the outlines of his campaign plans, there were any number of us trying to discourage a GOP emphasis on character.

By early June, it was apparent that unless a Whitewater smoking gun showed up by Labor Day, President Clinton would not be dented by the "character issue." The electorate knew exactly what it had in Bill Clinton, and it was quite prepared to give him a second term no matter how many of his old friends became convicted felons: "The ordinary Republican mindset does not comprehend that the vast majority of the American people do not have the luxury of automatically choosing personality over policy – saints over sinners.

Clinton and Character

As it stands, they would rather ride out the balance of the century with Clinton and gridlock than turn the government over to Dole-Gingrich. With both the Senator and the Speaker announcing over the weekend that the party's highest priority in this election year will be a promise to balance the budget, they leave the electorate no choice. A week or two ago, it still seemed possible that Bob Dole would be able to establish his footing as the candidate who would put growth above all other considerations, but the last several days have discouraged that hope. The very idea of scheduling one more vote on a constitutional amendment to balance the budget, as his Senate swan song, reminds the electorate that Dole is about pessimism, austerity and the past."[1]

There was a sense among Democrats of a tightening race between the President and Dole. This was only because they genuinely fear the voters will become thoroughly disgusted with Clinton and the character issue as the felony convictions of his friends mount. Ted Van Dyk, an Establishment Democrat who worked for Hubert Humphrey in the old days, startled the readers of *The Wall Street Journal* on Monday, June 3, by warning that the President might actually be forced to resign. His op-ed essay was disguised as contingency planning, in the event the President loses the capacity to govern in the same way his protégé – Arkansas Governor Jim Guy Tucker – lost his the previous week. Van Dyk, who is close to Vice President Al Gore, suggested we mentally prepare ourselves for a Gore candidacy. *New York Times* columnist William Safire the previous week suggested that President Clinton should think of "flipping" the Clinton-Gore ticket to Gore-Clinton, to dilute the character issue. "The grapevine is abuzz with wild speculation about what to expect next. Tongues are wagging in every world capital about the possibility that there is a Whitewater smoking gun working its way to the surface, and that a Clinton resignation may

---

1 Jude Wanniski, "Dole, Taxes and the Character Issue," Polyconomics, Inc., Morristown, N.J., June 4, 1996.

wind up being the flip side of the Nixon resignation. In a way, the symmetry suggests a settling of scores within the political Establishment. It is no coincidence that *The Wall Street Journal* has been as rabid in its pursuit of Clinton as *The Washington Post* and the *NY Times* were in bringing down RMN over a two-bit Watergate burglary."[2]

It helped enormously that the stock market was then booming, while it was in a horrible decline at the time of Nixon's Watergate. Clinton should be able to campaign right up to November 5 with every prospect of winning re-election. "Even if every person who votes for him wishes they didn't have to, it will not turn the election to Bob Dole. When you note that only 7 percent of black Americans have a positive opinion of Newt Gingrich and that 65 percent are negative, and that only 17 percent of women have a positive opinion of him, for example, you can understand why Dole will not close the gap against Clinton. The poorer people are, the more anxious they are about their families and their futures, the more likely they will come out to vote for Clinton in November. It was this anxiety vote that turned out in November 1986 to take the U.S. Senate away from the Republicans, worried that the last two years of the Reagan White House might be tough on those with no cushion to see them through."[3]

Grass-roots Republicans were not the problem. It was the party institution, as it had evolved in the last half century, forcing normally reasonable men like Newt Gingrich to lose perspective once he got his hands on the levers of power. On "Meet the Press" Sunday, June 3, when asked to cite the biggest mistake he made as Speaker, Gingrich humbly allowed that he erred in holding too many press conferences! He could not admit the substance of his work had been deeply flawed. He had to blame the electorate for not being smart enough to know how much good he tried to do for it. If only *he had not told the voters what he was doing*, he would be popular. For his

2 Ibid.

3 Ibid.

part, Bob Dole was even more deeply embedded in the kind of Republican orthodoxy that reached its zenith in Richard Nixon's truncated second term. "Dole's chief of staff, Sheila Burke, upon whom he relies, knows that Dole should not try to be someone he is not. She resists the pressures from those who are trying to turn him into an optimist, a tax-cutting Happy Warrior. Dole, though, clearly worries that the voters are not interested in the real Dole, which he would prefer to be."[4]

As these arguments against the President's character built further among Republican opinion leaders, one had to wonder what he would look like stripped completely of questions of ethics, morals or personal idiosyncrasies. It was plain that "the Beltway Republicans and their friends in the media had persuaded themselves that Bill Clinton would be defeated by Dole because the American people would reach a critical mass of disgust with the mountain of evidence that Bill and Hillary belong to neither the Boy Scouts nor the Girl Scouts. The electorate, though, did not hire Bill Clinton in 1992 primarily to provide a role model for their sons, nor Hillary for their daughters."[5] It was much more complicated. Though the conservative Republicans would have the electorate believe so, it is probably not the job of the commander in chief to provide moral leadership. Better to leave that position to the Reverend Billy Graham. "The President's job is to guide the executive branch on domestic and foreign policies that would serve the best interests of the nation. In his first two years, he did a rather poor job of trying to interpret the 'mandate' given him by only 43 percent of the vote in a three-way race with George Bush and Ross Perot. Yet he didn't do much damage. The Republican minority in Congress was adroit enough to block his health-care initiatives. And the President wisely stayed on the good side of Fed Chairman Alan Greenspan, which counts for a lot."[6]

---

4 Ibid.

5 Jude Wanniski, "In Defense of the President," Polyconomics, Inc., Morristown, N.J., July 2, 1996.

6 Ibid.

The 1993 tax increase, which Clinton pushed through Congress without a single Republican vote – but with Greenspan's passive assent – was his worst move, but I noted he had apologized publicly for that. In foreign affairs, his *ad hoc* approach had worked better than the country had any right to expect. The world did seem to be mending itself on the margins and in a bit better shape than it was four years earlier. Mexico was an exception, with the Clinton Treasury helping push it into a peso devaluation and a steep fall in its economy and the living standards of its people. Otherwise, the administration's foreign economic policy was okay, its bark always worse than its bite. Global financial markets have been grateful. With this experience, it was fairly safe to assume that a second Clinton term would be better than his first and the U.S. financial markets seemed to agree, particularly with Alan Greenspan firmly in place at the Fed. Although the GOP might lose the House in November, it almost certainly would remain in control of the Senate, with Trent Lott in position at least to make marginal improvements in the tax code. In foreign affairs, the President had run up the learning curve and had a seasoned team in place. There was much less chance of another Mexico and less risk of a breakdown on trade with Japan or China, now that the U.S. and its trading partners had become accustomed to the Clinton parameters. The G-7 meeting in Lyons, France, during the June 29 weekend had been dismissed as merely a photo-op for the President, but he clearly had earned the respect of his global counterparts. They were not only grateful that he had so far effectively brought order to Bosnia, their own backyard, but also that he had not done anything to precipitate a global recession. In sum:

> This is not the record of a President who can be pitched out of office by Bob Dole – either on the grounds that he did not manage his finances or libido to high standards while Governor of Arkansas, or that he did not run a tight ship at the White House after he arrived from Little Rock.

The public opinion polls indicate Bob Dole is the choice of only 5 percent of African Americans in a matchup with Clinton and that he draws only about a third of the women's vote. There is no way Dole can close the gender gap by policy speeches, campaign advertising or selection of a woman as his running mate. Women and minorities are afraid of Bob Dole because they see in him a Cold Warrior who wants to balance the budget – which is what he is, for goodness sakes. After a 30-year decline in real wages that paralleled the sacrifices of the Cold War, the people at the bottom of the socio-economic pyramid have *to be frightened* by a candidate who: 1) pledges to expand military outlays to confront the hostile world he envisions; 2) threatens to enlarge NATO in order to isolate Russia as a means of stoking that hostility; and 3) vows to balance the budget no matter what it takes. It does not matter how much any of us might prefer Dole to Clinton in the Oval Office, if only to avoid reading about Paula Jones or Hillary's New Age paganism. Ordinary Americans are thoroughly justified in fearing a Dole presidency.[7]

One of the first things made clear when Dole announced his choice for Vice President was that Kemp would not undertake the role of "attack dog" or "pit bull," roaming the country cataloging the myriad allegations, innuendoes and actual scandals that had rocked the Clinton administration. To those in the party who wanted to beat the President on these issues, Kemp's refusal to take the low road became a constant irritant as the campaign plowed forward with no sign that the high road could close the gap. It was not that Kemp was squeamish about going negative. He believed, as did the consensus on the Dole campaign from the top down, that it would be the economic issues Kemp brought to the ticket that were the

---

7 Ibid.

only chance of winning – short of a scandalous smoking gun that had not appeared. On June 18, three weeks before he was chosen by Dole, Kemp appeared on the Chris Matthews CNBC "Politics" show and was asked about the relevance of the character issue. He dismissed it as a distraction, and pointed out that the Bush campaign had relied upon it in the 1992 campaign when it was deployed against a Bill Clinton unknown to the national electorate. If it did not work then, why would it work in 1996, with Clinton holding a 20-point lead in the polls despite four years of assaults on his character?

There were, of course, those in the campaign who were ready to go negative, as there always are. John Buckley, the communications director, was a primary advocate of the attack mode. According to a New York Times post-mortem, by the end of the campaign Dole had become persuaded that Buckley was the primary source of press reports of internal dissension on this issue and would no longer talk to him.[8] Immediately after the San Diego convention, the Dole media team of Don Sipple and Mike Murphy were dismissed as a result of an internal feud with Buckley. At the time, there was the possibility the new team of Paul Manafort and Rick Davis would be an improvement, as Sipple and Murphy were specialists in the art of the negative. It was Sipple and Murphy who produced the reprehensible Governor Merrill advertisements for Dole in New Hampshire. Alas, the Manafort-Davis team thereupon added Alex Castellanos, another negative specialist who achieved notoriety in the Jesse Helms 1990 Senate campaign with racially divisive TV spots against Helm's black Democratic opponent.

The effectiveness of negative advertising is a matter of debate. Its practitioners insist it works, and it undoubtedly does in certain types of campaigns and in certain circumstances. It is always going to work better when the voters are not familiar with the target's

---

8 Adam Nagourney and Elizabeth Kolbert, "How Bob Dole's Dreams Were Dashed," The New York Times, November 8, 1996, p. A1.

character, ideology or voting record. An investment in sharp attacks on an incumbent President who has been under a microscope for four years on the same points of contention was never likely to produce positive returns. The idea becomes even less attractive if the assumption is correct that Dole and Kemp had to present themselves as being less threatening and more reasonable than Newt Gingrich. The only kind of negative advertising that would be appropriate would be substantive attacks on policy issues where Clinton was vulnerable. There was never a point in the campaign where the Dole media team responsible for spending $60 million came close to producing a positive return with their ads. Those which identified Dole with a "balanced budget" or a hard line on crime simply reinforced those characteristics the voters already identified with Newt Gingrich. Did Kemp or anyone on his team have anything to say about the content of the paid media? Not a word.

I had hoped to at least be able to get my two cents in on the media campaign, because Kemp and Sears were technically inside the campaign and at least would bring me to the edge of it. My opinion of GOP "media experts" has always been extremely low, and it would become even lower as a result of this race. The reason they are *at best* only barely competent is that from their school days they "think Republican." That is, they are attracted to Republican politics because of their circle of family or friends. They never quite understand why anyone would want to be a Democrat. In one of my conversations with Steve Forbes years before we talked about him entering the political fray, I asked him if he understood the disadvantage he had in being born with a silver spoon in his mouth. I would never know what it was like to be born to wealth, but because I was born into a working class family and had climbed to a position of modest wealth, I at least had a sense of how things looked from either side of the tracks. I told Steve that he could only imagine the view from the bottom. The Dole pollster and media team never evinced the slightest understanding of the people on the other side of the line who they were trying to win over. They were simply slapping down templates that had worked in various races in their careers – for senator or governor or whatever – and hoping for the best.

This is why President Clinton was wise to look to Dick Morris for counsel after his first unsuccessful years in the White House, as Morris taught himself both sides of the partisan perspectives. This has been a problem of governance through all of history, with royal dynasties destructing because they assumed that if there is no bread, the masses should eat cake. Mark Twain's novel, *The Prince and the Pauper*, turns on this idea, with a young prince and his look-alike subject changing places and seeing things from the other's vantage point. In the same way, Democratic "media experts" are marginally superior than their conservative counterparts. Even when they have the worst side of a particular issue, they are better at warning their natural followers about how the Republicans can't be trusted. And Republicans can't win national elections unless they can win the trust of some part of the masses of ordinary people from the other side of the tracks. Ronald Reagan was a perfect example of a Democrat turned Republican, winning his campaigns because he understood GOP strengths and knew how to address the concerns of the blue-collar Democrats he grew up with as a boy. He was a good shepherd, a gentle but forceful one who would spur on the flock, but at least try to leave none behind.

When Sipple and Murphy were fired by Dole campaign manager Scott Reed, in the power play involving John Buckley, I thought perhaps some headway could be made with Paul Manafort and Rick Davis, the new team. Manafort, who was the overall manager of the San Diego convention, is one of John Sears's many political protégés. This gave me some hope I could get an oar in on the media effort. In addition, the Manafort-Davis media enterprise has as its financial backer one of my clients at Polyconomics, John Lakian. A Massachusetts real-estate developer who had run unsuccessfully for both governor and senator in the state, Lakian will readily admit that his media campaigns in both races were poorly run by GOP "media experts" and that he is to blame for allowing them to run the way they did.

As soon as it was reported that his partners were hired to run the Dole media campaign, Lakian called to tell me he was going to arrange a meeting with me and Rick Davis, who he assured me was a good guy. I recall telling an incredulous John Sears that we had a stroke of luck, and that I was going to be able to influence the shape of the media campaign via Lakian and Davis. A month later and several dozen telephone calls produced no such meeting, not even a telephone conversation. Lakian finally told me in total exasperation that Paul Manafort had made up his mind to run the media campaign "his own way." Lakian explained this would be to tear into Bill Clinton's character and policies. I'd written a long memo suggesting a different tack, again on the grounds that the voters now knew all about Clinton and any money spent on teaching them something new would be money wasted. The $60 million spent went down the rathole. A sizeable chunk of the television money actually cost Dole votes every time certain spots ran. One showed Clinton making a speech in Texas apologizing to the voters for having raised taxes more than he should have. I could not believe how dense these guys were, never realizing the voters who were upset at the 1993 Clinton tax increases might never have known that he apologized for them, which meant he might reverse them, unless they had seen the Dole spots. The message that came through was *the apology*, as it does take a certain amount of character to admit a mistake.

In the end, I came to think that President Clinton's human weaknesses were a positive contribution to his re-election. The voters might have subtracted points from Clinton on this account, but the real cost to the Republicans was the enormous amount of time, energy and money spent advertising what every American knew about Bill Clinton – which meant tiny resources left for trying to persuade the voters that Bob Dole would be a good fellow in the Oval Office.

CHAPTER SEVEN

An Alternative Strategy: The Left Flank

The Dole team did not have a strategy as much as it had a working concept of how their man could overtake the incumbent President. The concept was that if the voters only knew what a bad fellow the President was, via incredibly expensive TV advertising, the voters would rouse themselves from their stupor and rise up in outrage. Bob Dole watched the TV spots and campaign material his high-priced advisors ran by him, and he was clearly outraged. "Where's the outrage?" he asked in the terminal moments of his campaign. It never occurred to him that the TV spots had been produced for *him*, not the voters.

It was not as if the Kemp team did not attempt to coax the campaign into a different conceptual framework, a genuine strategy. From the earliest contacts between the two teams in San Diego, the Kemp team tried to sell the idea that Clinton and the Democrats should be attacked on their *left flank*. That is not as strange as it may seem when stated so baldly. Bob Dole's political mentor, Richard Nixon, had reminded Dole that *in the Republican primaries, you run to your right, and in the general election, you run to your left.* Because the President had spent two years chasing Gingrich further and further to the right, he had fortified his position both at the center and on his right, but remained vulnerable on the left. Dick Morris had advised the President to keep pushing Gingrich toward the right-wing cliff in the Michael Kinsley strategy of *confrontational accommodation.* In order to do this, Clinton had moved well off-center himself toward the right. There seemed to some of us an opening on the left flank.

An Alternative Strategy: The Left Flank

On domestic policy, running to Clinton's left would mean emphasizing economic growth over budget balancing, which the President had embraced as his own. On foreign policy, running to Clinton's left meant stressing diplomacy over the use of military force, an idea discussed further in Chapter Nine. The idea of hitting the Democratic left flank was generally met with raised eyebrows whenever it was mentioned during the campaign, as if it suggested some form of socialism. With six weeks left to campaign, that flank was still exposed. Tony Fabrizio was running things at this point. Fabrizio certainly was not alone in his insistence that the American people wanted the political center of gravity in Washington at the center-right, with his polls playing well with the Manafort-Davis media campaign. There was no strategy in this thinking, no concept of the forces at work in the American psyche given the Gingrich factor. "It does not take a rocket scientist to see that with President Clinton still [so far to the right], it would be better to be at his left than at his right."

When the President of the United States puts on a steel helmet and flak jacket and orders the bombing of a foreign country [Iraq] without checking with anyone but his toadies, he is well to the right of Jesse Helms and Strom Thurmond. When he announces that the economy cannot grow faster than $2\frac{1}{2}$ percent, the President is telling the entire base of the Democratic Party, colored black and brown, that this is as good as it gets. The President has moved so far right on fiscal policy that he now favors a *reserve army of unemployed.* Delighted that he is keeping wages from rising, the Fortune 500 have contributed megabucks to his favorite charity, the DNC. If there are any upward pressures on wages, Mr. Clinton assures us that Alan Greenspan, who represents the security of the bond market, will nip them in the bud. Hillary and Robert Reich promise that the unemployed will get free health care, college scholarships, and school uniforms. Treasury Secretary Bob

Rubin, who has his $100 million under lock and key, favors giving a capital gains tax only to poor people who invest in homes worth no more than $500,000. If you are at the bottom of the economic pile and are as happy as Fabrizio says you are, stick with Clinton-Gore.[1]

From the beginning, Kemp had no trouble selling Dole on the idea of going after the black vote. This would be the one clear break with traditional Republican presidential campaigns going back to 1960. The national Democratic Party in the 1950s was still heavily reliant on the Solid South and had to play to the segregationists in the New Deal coalition. At the same time, the national Republican Party still counted on a sizeable fraction of the black vote, which had shifted to the Democratic Party beginning with the 1936 presidential election as blacks migrated north during the Great Depression. In the 1960 campaign, John F. Kennedy made a strategic decision to fire up support for black causes, with open support of Martin Luther King's civil disobedience. Richard Nixon made a strategic decision to go in the other direction, taking the GOP into its "Southern Strategy" that aimed at breaking the Democratic Party's hold south of the Mason-Dixon line. From 1960 through 1992 – nine straight national elections – the GOP ticket actively avoided direct appeals to the black community. It did so on an assumption that became embedded in the thinking of GOP political advisors that for every black vote that might be gained, two white would be lost. There is no record that the national party spent any funds on paid media in the black community during all those years – neither black radio nor newspapers. GOP success in finally winning elections after the long drought from 1932 to 1952 was evidence enough to stick to the winning formula.[2]

---

1 Jude Wanniski, "The Old Man and the Polls," Polyconomics, Inc., Morristown, N.J., September 24, 1996.

2 Michael Tomasky, "A Raceless Race," *New York*, November 18, 1996, pp. 30-32.

An Alternative Strategy: The Left Flank

One of the reasons Kemp gave for his decision not to run for President in 1996 was his sense that, following the 1994 GOP victory in the off-year elections, the party's center of gravity had shifted away from his stress on economic growth toward a stress on cultural conservatism, one that would discount minority concerns. One exit poll reported that 62 percent of white, adult males had voted Republican, which the press corps immediately translated into "angry white males." California Governor Pete Wilson, a one-time supporter of affirmative action for blacks, read the polls and decided to run for President as the champion of the California Civil Rights Initiative, Proposition 209, which would end race-based affirmative action. Senator Phil Gramm of Texas read the polls too and came out swinging as an angry white male in his presidential bid.

On February 5, 1995, in an interview with Dole, CNN's Frank Sesno told him that Phil Gramm said the first thing he would do as President would be to end affirmative action. After a moment's hesitation, Dole said that also would be the first thing he would do. Why? Dole cited the 62 percent poll of white, adult males. Armstrong Williams, a black conservative talk-show host in Washington, D.C., and one of Dole's staunchest supporters, was shocked at Dole's response. Armstrong, a close friend of Justice Clarence Thomas and a good friend of mine, also opposed affirmative action, but he could not believe Dole would cite the white vote as his reason for changing his position from pro to con. Armstrong called me at my office the following day to report that his telephone was ringing off the hook from black friends who were rubbing his nose in Dole's CNN statement. I wrote a brief memo to Dole, warning of the implications of his insensitivity and Armstrong's reaction. My advice was to support a phasing out of the affirmative-action programs on the books instead of a cold-turkey approach, first eliminating those that had been most abused. If Dole had any chance of increasing his share of the minority vote, he could not be insisting that the few props to those at the bottom of the pile be pulled out before the national economy was growing rapidly enough to train and absorb them at a living wage. Dole might have understood this in the abstract, but determined not to allow the other GOP contenders to outflank him on his right, he ignored the warning and continued pounding away at simply ending affirmative action.

Dole had considerable standing in the black political community because of his flawless civil rights record, his support for affirmative action dating back to Nixon's Philadelphia Plan to open the construction trades to blacks, and the key role he played in making Martin Luther King's birthday a national holiday. Neither he nor his campaign staff seemed to understand how crass his maneuvering appeared to a national audience that was already paying attention. His national approval ratings began to sink almost immediately after this statement on affirmative action, followed by two decidedly unpresidential decisions he later tried to blame on his staff. One was the decision to return a $1,000 contribution to The Log Cabin Republicans, a gay organization; the other a rejection of an invitation to address the spring convention of the NAACP. In each of these cases, Dole was playing the kind of street politics that goes into a hard-nosed legislative campaign, in which you target your majority coalition and ignore all those who don't fit. The national electorate, which looks for inclusiveness in the one political leader who represents everyone, saw in Dole's behavior more of the divisiveness they had seen in Newt Gingrich's style of power devolution. In trying to recover from these blunders, Dole was much too obvious in trying to avoid the blame by throwing it on his staff. By contrast, when Clinton's chief staff advisor was forced to resign in a scandal with a prostitute, a horrendous blow to the President on the day he gave his acceptance speech at the Chicago convention, both he and Hillary called to commiserate with Dick Morris and made sure the call was made public. The political crowd scratched its head in wonderment when the President's popularity rose in the overnight tracking polls.

An Alternative Strategy: The Left Flank

If Dole had been a relative unknown, he could not have survived such blunders, but the solid foundation of his 35-year record in Congress on these issues counted heavily in his favor. Representative Charles Rangel, the Harlem Democrat with the greatest seniority of all black political leaders, a number of times in the course of the campaign made positive references to Dole's record "before he ran for President." In other words, Dole's decision to bring Kemp onto the ticket with him was probably sufficient to give Dole a second chance with the electorate in overcoming the bad vibrations in the earlier phase of his campaign. As a member of Congress, as HUD Secretary and as director of Empower America, Kemp practically made a political career out of trying to bring black Americans and other minorities into the GOP. On the other hand, at the San Diego convention, Kemp had to "adjust" his own public positions on the California initiatives involving affirmative action and illegal immigration to fit the Dole stance and the GOP platform. John Sears made it plain to Kemp on day one that he had no other choice. A running mate could have no independent agenda on central issues. There was enough wiggle room in the rhetoric devised to permit Kemp to squeeze into the new posture with a clean conscience. California Attorney General Dan Lundgren, a Kemp friend from congressional days, helped out with opinions on how the initiatives could be administered with civility and compassion. Still, Kemp had to expect and did get beat up by Democrats and their journalist friends for "abandoning principle."

To have any realistic chance of winning, given the original Gingrich problem, the Dole-Kemp ticket had to break into the black vote, which in early August was showing only 5 percent for Dole. In San Diego, Kemp began talking about getting 25 percent of that vote, which pollster Fabrizio dismissed as highly improbable, but allowed that if it happened, Dole would in fact win. In one of the team's first campaign swings together, they traveled to Nashville where Kemp introduced Dole to a national convention of black journalists. This time Kemp and Sears got to massage the speech and Dole delivered one of his best of the campaign on Friday, August 23. If nothing else, he was reaching out to a new constituency. It ought to have been the dawning of a brave new world, but it wasn't. Nevertheless, Dole had been extraordinary. But to win the race, it could not be the last speech he made to a black audience.

> Black Americans have developed a cynicism about Republicans that can't be overcome simply by putting out a welcome mat. Your aggressiveness in making that point struck exactly the right note...This can't be the last speech you make to blacks. Sending Jack as a surrogate does not do the job...It means advertising on black media – your voice going into black homes on gospel and rap stations, your message written in print ads in black community newspapers...
>
> You are contesting for the *leader of the national family – the top of the power pyramid.* If you come across as the Father of the Old Testament, you will lose. If you come across as the Father of the New Testament, you will win. It is as simple as that.[3]

Kemp did make several additional speeches to black audiences, in Los Angeles, Chicago, New York and Northern New Jersey. Political journalists such as Walter Shapiro of *USA Today* and Chris Matthews of CNBC expressed amazement that Kemp would make speeches about healing the racial divide before all-white audiences in the Southern states. On the other hand, anonymous quotes appeared here and there in criticism of Kemp wasting his time on the effort, at times even from unnamed aides within the Dole campaign. The Dole schedulers tried to encourage Kemp to go into white, ethnic sections of the inner cities instead of the black sections,

---

3 Jude Wanniski, Memo to Bob Dole, August 24, 1996.

but Kemp frequently insisted on making stops in the black sections anyway. He always had Dole's full support. On the other hand, despite all the talk about spending some of the $61 million handed the campaign by Uncle Sam on black media, not one dime was spent. The only opening left in this area would have to come in free publicity, which Kemp inadvertently initiated with an interview with *The Boston Globe's* Mike Rezendes on September 8, with a page one headline: "Muslims' Self Help Praised by Kemp."

CHAPTER EIGHT

The Farrakhan Initiative

On the weekend prior to the October 16, 1995, Million Man March, I wrote a lengthy analysis of what was about to happen and predicted it would be a great success for the black community in general and Nation of Islam leader Louis Farrakhan in particular. At that point, I'd had absolutely no contact with the NOI, but Jack Kemp had met Minister Farrakhan's chief-of-staff and son-in-law, Leonard Muhammad. As Secretary of Housing and Urban Development in the Bush administration, Kemp had major responsibilities for inner city matters. In his four years, he no doubt shook hands with more black and Hispanic men and women than the rest of the White House and Cabinet combined. He was the man Bush sent to Los Angeles during the riots that followed the controversial acquittal of the policemen who had clubbed a black man, Rodney King, with the beating videotaped by a bystander.

During the riots, an old friend from his football days, Hall-of-Fame Cleveland Brown halfback Jim Brown, called Kemp and suggested he meet with the NOI people, the only people who had the respect of the inner-city blacks. This is how he met with Leonard Muhammad, a Chicago businessman who had been born dirt poor on an Alabama farm some fifty years ago. He had succeeded in a "Popeye" fast-food franchise, become one of the nation's "Top 100 Black Republicans" in the Nixon years, married Donna Farrakhan, and joined the NOI full time to put it on a sound financial footing. It was Leonard Muhammed who escorted Kemp into the Los Angeles riot area to calm things down. In the Kemp years at HUD, several contracts were signed with the Nation to provide security at federal housing projects, which the "Black Muslims," as they were called, could do successfully even though unarmed.

The Farrakhan Initiative

My analysis at the time of the Million Man March focused on the *masculinity* of Farrakhan's message as well as his Islamic religion. For 400 years, the black man in America had been emasculated, first by slavery, then by a welfare system that substituted government for the male's role as family provider. My sense was that Farrakhan was neither bigoted nor anti-Semitic, despite the interpretation of some of his comments directed occasionally at the politics of Jews and Christians. As a faith, Judaism was of no help to the problems of the emasculated black male, for while it is patriarchal and masculine in its social bent ("an eye for an eye"), it is exclusive to its own lineage and has been essentially patronizing in its considerable help to black Americans. That is, they viewed blacks as victims of social injustice not dissimilar to the anti-Semitism by which the dominant power structure made Jews to feel second-class citizens. Yet the sympathy was that of a father to a child.[1] Over the centuries, Christianity, a matriarchal "mother church," has counseled turning the other cheek and salvation in the next world. Islam, as an offshoot of Judaism and Christianity, offers a faith that has here-and-now relevance to black Americans. The Nation of Islam, founded in 1930 in Chicago at the dawn of the Great Depression and the great black migration from South to North, provided that relevance.

On the night of the march, Farrakhan appeared on the "Larry King Live" show and rejected the anti-Semitic charge, telling King cryptically, "I am a Jew," by which he meant Islam's ecumenical embrace of the laws of Abraham and Moses. He also repeated a readiness to sit down with leaders of the Anti-Defamation League, the Jewish organization with which he has most been at sword

---

1 At a Polyconomics conference in early March 1997, Minister Farrakhan told an audience that included several Jewish clients that there was no question that of all white Americans, Jewish Americans were of the greatest political assistance to blacks in the first several decades, but it has always been as adults to children. The relationship must change, he said, but the Jewish political establishment resists the idea. "It is like parents who don't want their 45-year-old son to leave home because they don't think he can take care of himself," he said.

point. Asked if it were true that he was a black separatist, Farrakhan said he had little other choice – that black leaders had been trying to integrate into the white world for 400 years without success. His style of "separation" is not to move to a black enclave, but to stop *trying* to integrate with whites and focus on self-help instead.

I sent Kemp a tape of the three-hour speech to the marchers and a report on what Farrakhan had said to Larry King, urging that he step into the vacuum in an attempt to bridge the gap between the NOI and the Jewish community. Kemp was sufficiently impressed to make contact with Jim Brown, to make sure this was not all talk, and Brown assured him that the Farrakhan offer had been made in good faith. Kemp then called Abe Foxman of the ADL and asked of the possibilities of brokering a meeting of the two, with reconciliation the objective. Foxman told him such a meeting was impossible unless it were preceded by apologies from Farrakhan for everything he had ever said that was critical of Jews. Kemp decided to do nothing more, as I told him there was no chance Farrakhan would agree to preconditions of the magnitude demanded by Foxman. President Jimmy Carter could never have successfully brought together Israeli Prime Minister Menachim Begin and Egyptian President Anwar Sadat at Camp David if either of them demanded full apologies from the other before sitting down to talk of reconciliation. There the matter sat until Jack gave his interview ten months later to Mike Rezendes of the *Globe*.

The interview, datelined New York, began this way: "Jack Kemp, the self-styled Republican ambassador to minorities and the poor, believes Nation of Islam leader Louis Farrakhan's self-help philosophy is 'wonderful,' and rues the Republican Southern strategy for winning the White House in elections past as a 'shameful' tactic that divided blacks and whites."

'It's not the Republican base, but it should be,' Kemp said, when asked why he was campaigning in neighborhoods where Republicans routinely receive 10 percent or less of the vote. 'It's not good for America to have one party taking the black vote for granted and the other party writing it off.' Kemp was careful to say he does not endorse all the teachings of Farrakhan, who has been labeled anti-Semitic and who recently was barred by the US Treasury Department from receiving $1 billion in aid and a $250,000 humanitarian award from Libyan leader Moammar Khadafy.

But Kemp also said he so admired the Million Man March organized by Farrakhan last year, and the speech Farrakhan delivered at the event, that he wished he had been able to take part.

'That Million Man March was a celebration of responsible fatherhood, individual initiative, of not asking the government to do everything for you, and getting an opportunity to be the man that God meant you to be,' Kemp, 61, said. 'I would have liked to have been invited to speak.'

Rezendes said Kemp, "one the few nationally recognized Republicans to consistently focus on the problems faced by minorities and the poor, acknowledged the risk he was taking in praising Farrakhan's emphasis on black self-reliance and family values. 'I'm going to set off rockets if this is taken out of context,' Kemp said, 'but I think it is interesting that in America today, in the black community, more and more black church leaders are telling men to be responsible fathers and to be respectful of their wives and women.'[2]

The interview, which came spontaneously from Kemp without prompting from any of his friends, did set off rockets. *The New York Times* the next day carried a story about it, and as it happened Kemp was scheduled to speak that night in New York City at a gathering of the twelve most important U.S. Jewish leaders. Robert Novak's column a few days later noted: "Jack Kemp was stunned by the icy

---

2 Mike Rezendes, "Muslims' Self-Help Praised by Kemp," *The Boston Globe*, September 8, 1996, p. A1.

reception in New York from prominent Jewish leaders who were furious that a few days earlier he had complimented the 'self-help' elements of Black Muslim leader Louis Farrakhan's Million Man March. In a speech to the Conference of Presidents of Major Jewish Organizations, the Republican vice presidential candidate called on Farrakhan to renounce anti-Semitism. But his listeners responded in cold silence. At the same meeting, they applauded and cheered Kemp's Democratic rival, Vice President Al Gore. The normally ebullient Kemp was stunned by the reaction in New York from the organization that has warmly embraced him in the past. He has been an unvarying supporter of Israel, and, until now, the favorite Republican of Jewish leaders."[3]

The Washington Post's Richard Cohen, an avowed admirer of Kemp, went ballistic in his column that week. He asked: "How can a man of some erudition – and Kemp is one – not notice that when he parses Farrakhan, separating the good from the bad, he only is mimicking the fools who said Mussolini made the trains run on time, and Hitler – down deep – was nothing but a nationalist who advocated strong family values...It's a good thing Kemp did not talk at the Million Man March. He has done quite enough talking already."[4]

The Weekly Standard, a new Beltway political periodical founded by media mogul Rupert Murdoch, edited by William Kristol and, at the time, John Podhoretz, the sons of the most prominent Jewish intellectuals of our era,[5] chipped in with an editorial, which left Kemp no room for success in his initiative. How Farrakhan responded to Kemp, if he did, would not matter: "The impossibility of unraveling the anti-Semitic and the self-help elements of such an

---

3 Robert Novak, "Inside Report," *New York Post,* September 15, 1996, p. 39.

4 Richard Cohen, "Kemp's Condescension," *The Washington Post,* September 13, 1996, p. A29.

5 Kristol is the son of Irving Kristol, the neo-conservative author and scholar, and Bea Kristol, a historian. Podhoretz is the son of Norman Podhoretz, retired editor of the *Commentary,* the Jewish monthly, and Midge Decter, an editor and political activist. The four have been friends of Kemp and mine for 20 years.

event [the march] should be self-evident, but it wasn't to Kemp, who did call on Farrakhan to renounce his anti-Semitism two days after the *Globe* piece appeared."[6]

What might Kemp get out of this initiative? The impact of the possible political payoff was enormous: "Those of you who are already counting the Dole-Kemp ticket hopeless, with nine long weeks left to go, should consider Jack Kemp's latest contribution to the campaign. It has the potential of cracking the campaign open to a completely new level of debate."[7]

If the Dole-Kemp ticket was going to win in November, it would have to get 25 percent of the black vote. It could not succeed merely by running negative TV ads to tell the American people what a bad fellow Bill Clinton is: "Dole can't win with women voting 60-to-30 Clinton, and black women voting 99-to-1 for Bill and Hillary. Every Dole TV spot that promises to throw more of their sons and daughters into jail instead of useful employment only widens the gender gap. White, male Republican political consultants are, as a rule, too dense to understand that when their female focus groups express a fear of crime and drugs, they do not want the President to put everyone behind bars after they have been killed and raped. They want everyone to have enough hope, growth and opportunity to behave themselves to begin with. Kemp understands this better than anyone else in the campaign, which is why the ticket has a chance of winning. The people who will benefit most from a Dole-Kemp victory are African-Americans, female even more than male. But they don't yet believe it."[8]

To pay off, the Kemp initiative to broaden the Republican base in this revolutionary way first would have to produce a statement from

---

6 "Kemp's Farrakhan Problem," Editorial, *The Weekly Standard*, September 23, 1996, p. 3.

7 Jude Wanniski, "Kemp, Farrakhan and the Black Vote," Polyconomics, Inc., Morristown, N.J., September 10, 1996.

8 Ibid.

Farrakhan, in response to Kemp's challenge that he renounce anti-Semitism once and for all. The Minister of the Nation's New York City Mosque, Conrad Muhammad, who had been quoted in *The New York Times* about Kemp's views, believed there would be a positive response from Farrakhan at a speech for a black political convention in St. Louis, scheduled for September 28. The campaign was, of course, skittish about the whole affair. Unfortunately, September 28 came and went, with not a word in the media about Farrakhan's speech as it may have related to Kemp's challenge. The wire services that reported on Farrakhan's speech said nothing about Kemp. The *Chicago Tribune*'s reporter in St. Louis was silent as well. The initiative appeared to have failed. What happened? Conrad Muhammad did not know. At the last minute he had been unable to go to St. Louis.

Farrakhan had in fact positively answered the Kemp challenge in his St. Louis speech, but the press corps for some reason decided not to report on the event. Not until the October 22 issue of *The Final Call*, the weekly newspaper of the Nation of Islam, was it apparent that Kemp's gamble had been successful. A full page report announced: "**ANSWER TO CRITICS** – A response to comments made by **Jack Kemp – By Minister Louis Farrakhan**." An editor's note first explains that "contrary to some media misreports, the Honorable Minister Louis Farrakhan recently responded to comments made by Kemp." The text follows:

> When I was out of the country, the Vice Presidential candidate, Mr. Jack Kemp, said some kind words about Farrakhan and my work. He committed a cardinal sin, because you are not even allowed to recognize the good that God blesses me to do. Twelve presidents of the major Jewish organizations called Mr. Kemp on the carpet and beat him up. I think these are the same twelve presidents that met with Boutros Boutros-Ghali of the United Nations and told him that if he quieted down his criticism

of Israel when they were bombing Southern Lebanon they would guarantee that America would pay the U.N. the billion dollars that America owes. Mr. Clinton just went to the U.N. and promised to pay. Was that because of these twelve presidents? Well, don't beat up on Mr. Kemp.

I hope to come to New York. I would be glad to sit down with the twelve presidents. I don't think that they are the twelve disciples of Jesus. You don't have to talk about me. Talk to me. That is the manly thing to do. Jack Kemp said that he wanted Farrakhan and the Nation of Islam to denounce anti-Semitism. Let me say frankly, I denounce anti-Semitism in all its forms, and anybody who would hate Arabs, Jews, or any people because of their faith or color, I denounce that. It is easy for me to denounce anti-Semitism, because I know that in the eyes of God I am not that. I am critical of the conduct of some members of that community that ill effect my people and that ill effect this nation. I have a right to speak as I speak without being called anti-Semitic.

After all, there is none of us that are so sacred that we cannot be criticized. Particularly, if God says He makes all things new. He has justified why He makes all things new by condemning the things that presently exist. You criticize me and I don't call you anti-Black. I criticize government, but I am not anti-Government. I criticize America, but I am not anti-America. I criticize white people, but I am not anti-White. I criticize Arabs, but I am not anti-Arab. I criticize Blacks, but I am not anti-Black. I am critical of those things that God himself has Judged and Condemned and I want all of us to come into the favor of God. So, I cannot hold my tongue because you will feel offended. If something I say of truth steps on your toes, then straighten up your life. I am trying to straighten up mine so that we can come into the favor of God.

The Federal Reserve must come back under Congress. The IRS should either be abolished or altered and a proper taxing system should be set up. The mis-use of American soldiers for the greed of corporate America must cease.[9]

The statement was everything that Kemp had asked for, a personal vindication. He had asked for a renunciation of anti-Semitism from the most influential black leader in America and Farrakhan had done so emphatically, without reservation. Smack in the middle of the presidential campaign it was *news*, at the very least a feather in Jack's cap that would elevate his importance and influence in the Dole campaign. Yet there was not a word in the national news media about it. An inquiry confirmed that Farrakhan had actually answered Kemp's challenge in his St. Louis speech before 10,000 people. There were national reporters present, but none thought it newsworthy that Farrakhan had renounced anti-Semitism in the way he did. Or, that Farrakhan was responding directly to the challenge of the Republican vice-presidential nominee. Had Farrakhan responded negatively, the political press corps would certainly have taken note, adding to Kemp's burden of having stepped onto this dangerous ground. For the entire press corps to ignore the positive Farrakhan response was astonishing. A good part of the explanation was that the Dole campaign, which knew exactly what had happened, chose to ignore the opening rather than press the issue. The political press corps is so conditioned to being told what is news on the campaign plane that when nothing was said of the Farrakhan response, it was as if it did not happen.

Given what followed, though, this simple explanation was not enough to explain the dead silence of the entire political establishment about this *contretemps* between the Republican vice presidential nominee and the most influential black leader in America.

---

9 Minister Louis Farrakhan, "Answer to Critics," *The Final Call*, October 22, 1996, p. 4.

The Farrakhan Initiative

(A year later, *Time* listed Farrakhan as among the 25 most influential American leaders and *Vanity Fair* listed him as one of the 65 most influential leaders in the world.) The Farrakhan statement was out on Friday, October 11, and I immediately called both the Dole and Kemp offices in Washington to report what I took to be good news.

I told Leonard Muhammed how pleased I was to see the statement. He said that Minister Farrakhan had also telephoned the leaders of the Anti-Defamation League and the American Jewish Committee to offer to sit down with them personally on his visit to New York. Abe Foxman, the ADL director, had refused the offer, he said, while the Jewish Committee executive was still considering it. The theme of the UN Plaza event would be *reconciliation* among nations, and it seemed reasonable that in the spirit of his Kemp statement, Farrakhan would make this gesture to his most ardent adversaries in the Jewish community. This would please Kemp enormously. It should have impressed the Dole campaign as well. I told Leonard Muhammed I was coming into the city on Monday, to meet with Seth Lipsky, a friend of many years who is publisher of *The Forward*, an English-language Jewish weekly, to discuss the Farrakhan statement.

Finding Leonard Muhammed free for dinner that same night, I suggested we meet with Ted Forstmann, whose opinion would carry weight with Dole and Kemp. A maverick investor who had amassed a fortune buying companies that were diamonds in the rough, Forstmann is a keen judge of character, a friend of Kemp's and an avid supporter of the Dole-Kemp ticket. I knew my word would be insufficient to report on the meeting, but that Forstmann's would be taken seriously. Forstmann came away from the dinner pleasantly surprised by Leonard Muhammed's presentations. He passed that word on to the campaign, which helped in maintaining its interest in the possibility of a last-minute sign from Farrakhan to support the GOP ticket.

One of the things Leonard Muhammed confided at this October 14 dinner was that he and Farrakhan several weeks earlier had met

with Edgar Bronfman, the Seagram's whiskey king and head of the
World Jewish Congress, in his New York City apartment. He said the
dinner was a great success and that Bronfman had promised to arrange
a meeting with the same group of twelve Jewish presidents which
Kemp had addressed in September. He said he and Farrakhan hoped
it would soon bear fruit. The meeting with Bronfman had been
arranged by Mike Wallace of CBS' 60 Minutes, who had interviewed
Farrakhan earlier in the year and had been impressed by his earnest-
ness in seeking reconciliation with the Jewish community. That initiative later blew up when Wallace was premature in claiming it as a
success in a *Playboy* interview.[9] Wallace told me he did not realize the
Playboy editors would check with Bronfman because of the amount
of money Seagram's spent on advertising. When the December issue
hit the mails in the first days of November, the interview had been
doctored to indicate failure of the dinner meeting instead of success.
Bronfman, who was obviously not prepared to have it known that he
and Minister Farrakhan were trying to find a path to reconciliation,
issued a statement to the Jewish press on November 5. Unable to
deny the meeting as it was reported by *Playboy*, Bronfman instead
simply denounced Farrakhan as "evil personified."[10]

Even so, time had run out on this attempt to encourage a shift in
the black vote, although I now was certain that this wedge in the
black community could divide its vote in future elections, breaking
the Democratic lock. If the Farrakhan statement of September 28
denouncing anti-Semitism had been widely publicized, there might
have been enough time to assure the electorate that it was genuine

---

9 Peter Ross Range, "Interview," *Playboy*, December 1996, p. 51.

10 Gerald Kahn, "How Bronfman Broke Bread with Rev. Louis Farrakhan," *The
Forward*, November 15, 1996, p. 1. Bronfman based his "evil personified" assertion on a speech Farrakhan made in Brooklyn two days after their dinner with
Mike Wallace. Farrakhan cited a *New York Times* report of the United Nations that
the economic sanctions against Iraq had caused the deaths of 500,000 Iraqi children. Farrakhan was quoted telling his Brooklyn audience that this was a
"Holocaust." Mike Wallace told me Mrs. Bronfman called him to complain that
this was "anti-Semitic." Still, Minister Farrakhan did not learn Bronfman thought
he was "evil personified" until he saw the news account in *The Forward* months later.

and that Kemp had played an instrumental role in beginning a process of national reconciliation. By October 16, the day of the UN Plaza event, the only news accounts of Farrakhan's offer to meet with Jewish leaders were by columnists of the *New York Daily News* and *New York Post*. There was no help there, as they denounced Farrakhan for making the offer and praised the Jewish leaders for rejecting it. My meeting with Seth Lipsky and other editors of the *Forward* was not productive. Lipsky did ask me to write an op-ed essay on Kemp and Farrakhan, explaining what we were trying to do, and I agreed. When I presented the essay a few days later, Lipsky called to say he just could not use it. I had simply argued that Farrakhan was now seriously seeking reconciliation with the Jewish community and the rest of the nation because his followers want him to:

> With the end of the Cold War, there is in our country and around the world an expectation of a peacetime economic expansion. This was the message Farrakhan tried to convey at the UN Plaza this week. In economic expansions, anti-Semitism always recedes, which is just one good reason why the forces of growth must be encouraged. My recommendation to my Jewish friends and opinion leaders is they take this chance on reconciliation. Jack Kemp has, knowing it would cause him considerable grief. If the Nation of Islam now turns on Jack, its leaders seem to know it would be the last time they would get that chance.

It seemed Farrakhan was simply radioactive in the Jewish community and the risks of getting into his vicinity were too high for a small newspaper to take. A few days later, I happened to be on a TV business show with Mortimer Zuckerman, owner-publisher of the *New York Daily News, The Atlantic Monthly*, and *U.S.News & World Report*. Off camera, I discussed the situation with Zuckerman, thinking he was big enough to resist pressures of the kind faced by Lipsky. It soon became clear he was not willing to be part of any initiative, and in fact acknowledged that a year earlier he had been visited by Leonard Muhammad, asking for help in this area, but that he just couldn't do it. On every front, apparently, the Jewish political establishment viewed Farrakhan not as an American black leader, but as an American black *Islamic* leader. As a black, he posed no threat to Jewish political influence in Washington, but as a black Muslim he was seen as a threat to Israel through the votes of the black community.

At the time, it seemed another missed opportunity for the Dole-Kemp ticket. Again and again Kemp offered the opinion on how *winnable* the race seemed to be. The idea behind the Farrakhan initiative never involved the expectation that there would be a formal endorsement from the NOI minister. If Dole and Kemp could be seen bringing a sense that their administration would be in a position to solve the racial divide, it would cut against the Gingrich factor. There might be a swing of a few percentage points in the black community if the initiative worked, but we surmised there would be a swing of a few points in the white community as well. The most powerful black leader in America – a man who could get a million men to come to Washington at their own expense on behalf of a social cause – was practically telegraphing his preference of Dole and Kemp versus the Democratic ticket.

There was enough give from Farrakhan for Dole-Kemp to claim they had succeeded in bringing the controversial black leader into the mainstream. His renunciation of anti-Semitism and bigotry would, of course, be ridiculed by the Democrats and the Jewish Establishment, but if the GOP campaign had made a big deal out of it, it is hard to see how the national electorate would be anything but impressed by what Kemp's initiative had produced. Had the conservative press celebrated the Farrakhan statement as a credit to Kemp, Dole would have been able to jump in to praise this break-through in a national reconciliation process. But there was almost complete silence. The lack of time and the reluctance of Republican opinion leaders and intellectuals to see any percentage in the "black vote" doomed the effort. As it happened, the black vote, which had registered as low as 5 percent for the GOP early in the year, gave 12 percent to Dole-Kemp, scarcely up from 11 percent for Bush-Quayle in 1992. The more interesting news was the sharp rise in the vote of black men. The Joint Center for Political and Economic Studies reported: "While there were equal numbers of black men and women voting in 1996 – approximately 4.79 million, that number represents a **decline** of about 300,000 for black women, and an **increase** of about 1.7 million for black men...[I]t seems likely that some significant portion of the increase must be attributed to the Million Man March of October 1995."

Why was there such resistance to Kemp's initiative among Republican opinion leaders – especially the editors of conservative newspapers and periodicals? There are many good answers wrapped up in the frostiness in this community to Kemp's general wooing of the black vote. The part that I think matters most is the central assumption that no matter what they do, the energy and resources will outstrip any possible gains. There is also the assumption that the price of black votes will always involve more government spending on social programs. This assumption is wrong. The *masculinity* of the Nation of Islam is punctuated by the statement of Minister Farrakhan's mentor, the late Elijah Muhammad: *We must say farewell to welfare.*

The social philosophy of the Nation of Islam clearly fits comfortably within the growth wing of the Republican Party. On a "Fox News Sunday," November 30, 1997, Farrakhan told interviewer Tony Snow that he believed the black community would benefit if its vote could divide equally between the two parties instead of being ignored by Republicans and taken for granted by Democrats. This force was contained in the 1996 campaign, but it will be harder to stop in 2000. It is, of course, in the interest of the Democratic Party to prevent a significant exodus of black and brown votes, but it is politically inevitable if the GOP continues its evolution as the party of entrepreneurial capitalism. Kemp's Farrakhan initiative came too late, but it gave the GOP something to think about.

CHAPTER NINE

Foreign Policy: Bombs Before Breakfast

*I*n the conventional post-mortems of the losing Dole-Kemp ticket, there is scarcely a word about foreign affairs. *Time* magazine's special election issue of November 18 said nothing about any differences on foreign policy between the candidates that may have contributed to the election outcome. *The New York Times'* extensive November 8 account of "How Bob Dole's Dreams Were Dashed" did not mention foreign affairs. In other accounts, a line or two appeared about Dole's differences with Clinton on California's referendum on illegal immigration, but that was about it. Why? It was not because there were not any critical issues confronting the world's only superpower that should have been debated in the presidential election. The plain and simple fact was that Bob Dole, from childhood in Kansas through U.S. Army service in the Second World War, had looked up to the President as commander-in-chief, automatically deserving of support on any matters that might involve putting a member of the armed forces in harm's way. The Republican presidents he served under – Nixon, Reagan and Bush – had his unequivocal support on foreign policy matters. He might chide a Democratic President on how to handle a brewing problem overseas, but even then his counsel invariably represented a consensus of the party establishment.

On the other hand, when President Clinton came to Washington fresh from the Arkansas statehouse, he had no distinct views on foreign policy. For the most part he simply turned himself over to the Democratic Party's pool of established practitioners in this area. Because the GOP had held the presidency for 20 of the previous 24 years, it was natural that both President Clinton and Bob Dole were drawing their views and opinions from the same central source. This source is essentially the Council on Foreign Relations and the senior members of the House and Senate committees on foreign relations. The Polaris or paradigm that had shaped and guided this bipartisan establishment was the Cold War. Robert Strauss, the Democrat who embodied bipartisanship beyond the water's edge in this period – the U.S. Ambassador to Moscow in the Bush adminis-tration and one of Dole's closest Democratic friends – arranged the first private lunch between Clinton and Dole soon after the 1993 inauguration. Thereafter, even Dole's slight criticisms of the admin-istration's foreign-policy decisions were almost designed to help the President, by adopting a tougher negotiating posture in "good cop, bad cop" situations with Bosnia, North Korea and China.[1]

A dozen years younger than Dole and a small boy during World War II, Jack Kemp had not been as trained to give unconditional support to the commander-in-chief. He also had been thinking about the post-Cold War world in terms of foreign economy policy for several years, while Dole had not. In wartime, everything is sub-ordinate to winning the war. In peacetime, the economy comes to the top of the electorate's agenda. In his 1979 book, *An American Renaissance,* Kemp devoted a chapter to the idea of "Exporting the American Dream," which outlined a way to extend entrepreneurial capitalism around the world based on supply-side economics. In the spring of 1987, as Kemp was making his preparations for an '88 bid for the GOP presidential nomination, he assembled a dozen of

---

1 In the two years, 1993 and 1994, when I was advising Dole privately, he was open to several of my suggestions on foreign economic policy, but not when national security was involved. He criticized the administration's support of "shock ther-apy" in Russia. He gave his quiet assent to my unsuccessful, private diplomacy with Cuba, which I had undertaken at the request of Representative Charlie Rangel [D-NY]. At my suggestion, Dole urged a "fact-finding mission" to Haiti prior to any military invasion, and added my advice that Colin Powell be included in order to talk to the generals. I was also among those who advised him on the Mexico peso crisis in early 1995.

his political advisors for a lunch and brainstorm session in a private room at the Republican Capitol Hill Club and for four hours talked grand strategy. My recommendation was that Jack run as an *internationalist*, who would secure the post-Cold War peace that was evident on the horizon.

The group appreciated my sentiments in that we were all frustrated by the foreign economic policies of the Reagan White House and Treasury, which simply deferred to the International Monetary Fund and the World Bank. Still, the assembled group was unanimous in opposing my recommendation, on the argument that it had never been done before. As the saying goes, *All politics is local*, and no candidate for the presidency had ever put the world ahead of the locals. It was decided that Kemp would run as a candidate who could be trusted to deepen and extend the *domestic* economic policies of Reagan. On foreign policy, Kemp would simply take a harder line with the communist adversaries than would Bush.

My private counsel to Kemp in early 1988, before the first primaries, was that inasmuch as Vice President George Bush was the only one of the eight GOP candidates who was completely in support of President's Reagan's peace initiatives with Moscow and Mikhail Gorbachev, it was unlikely the GOP would deny Bush the nomination. Kemp's biggest applause line on foreign policy was that he would *never negotiate new agreements with the Soviet Union until they lived up to their past agreements*. I told him to ignore the enthusiastic applause, which was worthy of a member of Congress, but not the presidency. The national electorate would always want their President to be open to negotiations with foreign adversaries. Peaceful reconciliation of differences is always preferable to war, especially between nuclear superpowers.[2] As long as the Vice President campaigned in complete support of Reagan policies, foreign and domestic,

---

2 After his unsuccessful primary campaign, Kemp hosted a lunch at the Capitol Hill Hyatt to thank a few hundred of his campaign team and financial supporters. When asked about mistakes he thought he had made, he mentioned the line about not negotiating with the Soviets until they lived up to their past agreements.

he could not be denied the nomination. With his foreign policy credentials and his "read my lips, no new taxes" pledge, Bush never had to break a sweat in his race with Massachusetts Governor Michael Dukakis, the 1988 Democratic nominee.

As it turned out, the electorate's decision was good. Bush assembled a solid foreign policy team, with James Baker III at State, Richard Cheney at Defense, and General Colin Powell at the Joint Chiefs of Staff and then National Security Advisor. The Cold War ended peacefully in 1990 and Germany was reunited. George Bush was no longer necessary for wartime duty, and as he simultaneously broke his "read my lips" pledge on taxes, it seemed he almost did not *want* to be re-elected. When the Berlin Wall came down, Bush turned the keys to the world over to Colin Powell and headed for his golf cart in Kennebunkport. As the recession in the national economy deepened at the grass roots, the President was conducting his press conferences from his golf cart, assuring the country that all was well. In 1992, he had to struggle more than expected to win the GOP nomination again, with Pat Buchanan putting up a spirited challenge over the breaking of the "no new taxes" pledge. Had Bush kept his pledge, it is fairly clear there would have been no recession, and neither Buchanan nor Ross Perot would have entered the race.[3] In addition, President Bush's successful conclusion of the Gulf War did not seem to help him in the realm of foreign policy. His brief popularity soon transferred to General Powell, upon whom Bush had relied in the conduct of the war. Americans credited Powell above all other Bush advisors, and even the President himself, for terminating the war when the Iraqi army had been expelled from Kuwait. I personally had no opinion of Powell, one way or the other, until it became clear, first in news accounts, then in his autobiography, that he had persuaded the President *not* to exterminate the

---

3 Jude Wanniski, "Blame Bush for the Recession," *The New York Times*, November 12, 1991, p. A25. I advised the "Reagan Democrats" and growth-oriented Republicans that they might as well start looking for a growth candidate in their own party, as it was unlikely Bush would be able to survive his tax increase.

Iraqi army and go into Baghdad to track down Saddam Hussein; my admiration for him shot up. It was also probably the chief source of his popularity with the mass of ordinary Americans.

The consensus of the dominant wing of the American foreign-policy establishment at the time was on the other side of the issue, supporting General Norman Schwartzkopf's effort to push the war into Baghdad. Powell had argued that the mission had been completed as far as the allied coalition was concerned, and that the "turkey shoot" of the 100,000 Iraqi Republican Guard in full retreat would cause great dismay among the Islamic members of the coalition.[4] Another fear was that if our troops cornered Saddam Hussein, he might have the capacity to inflict enormous casualties on them via chemical or biological weapons. The restraint shown at this point by President Bush caused widespread grumbling at the time by GOP opinion leaders and military strategists, but because the President's popularity rating rocketed above 90 percent, the grumbling was contained. The issue was revived in 1995 and 1996, though, when it appeared that Colin Powell's popularity might cut a swath to the Oval Office. The right wing of the GOP did not mind if Powell would wind up Secretary of State in a Dole administration, but it did not want to see a general with a relatively pacifist view of the post-Cold War world as President and commander in chief. Cleverly, the "wingers," as the right-wingers refer to themselves, attacked his candidacy not on his generalship, but on his support of the "pro-choice" side of the abortion issue.

The opening on the issue of President Clinton's competence as commander-in-chief seemed evident to me on September 3, hours after the traditional Labor Day kickoff of the presidential campaign.

---

4 Brent Scowcroft, who was President Bush's National Security Advisor, at the time leaned toward the idea of going to Baghdad. By 1996, he acknowledged that U.S. restraint in staying within the agreed-upon mission had greatly impressed the Islamic world. If we had broken our word and mowed down 100,000 young men in a turkey shoot, it would be a long, long time before the Islamic world would have gotten over the impulse to repay us with terrorist acts.

Foreign Policy: Bombs Before Breakfast

The President began with a bang, ordering the bombing of Iraq on the grounds that Saddam Hussein had sent Iraqi tanks into the "no-fly zone" of the Kurdish region in northern Iraq. No matter how conditioned Dole had been to saluting the commander-in-chief, President Clinton, in fact, had bombed a sovereign country with whom the United States was technically at peace. The President had not consulted *or informed* our Gulf War allies of our intent to bomb Iraq. Why? On the patently ridiculous grounds that Saddam had sent *ground troops into a no-fly zone in his own country.* Saddam had done this at the request of the duly constituted provincial Kurdish government, besieged by rebel Kurds, who were supported by Iran, the archenemy of Iraq and, of course, no friend of the United States. This was only the beginning. Not only did the President fail to consult or inform the relevant leaders of Congress before sending U.S. troops into harm's way, in blatant violation of the War Powers Act. He also did this after Dole had said it would be "premature" to take military action. And he did so hours after the leading members of the relevant House and Senate committees, whom he should have consulted, had said in nationally televised interviews that it was premature to drop bombs on Iraq, not knowing if Saddam Hussein had actually violated any rules by what he had done.[5]

Ross Perot was quickly on the wires with the wry comment that Clinton's action was designed to give him a bump in the polls, but that was all Perot said on the subject. R.W. Apple, Jr., the senior correspondent of *The New York Times*, was not fooled by Clinton's statement that it was in U.S. national interest to "slap Iraq." In his analysis published the day *prior* to the bombing, Apple said it was only because Saddam was "permanently demonized in the West by the Persian Gulf war" that Clinton could get away with bombing

---

5 The Sunday before President Clinton issued his order, the situation was discussed on the Sunday talk shows by Senator John Warner [R-VA] of the Armed Services Committee and Representative Lee Hamilton [D-OH], the ranking Democrat on House Foreign Affairs. Both were stern in discussing what Saddam had done, but were emphatic in saying it was premature to "drop iron bombs" on Iraq.

Iraq. Saddam, he said, was "in a far more credible position than when he sent his army racing into Kuwait, an independent country, or even when he stormed into northern Iraq five years ago to put down a rebellion." Apple added: "Purely in political terms of domestic politics, the call is a no-brainer...Inevitably the Administration will contend that the credibility of the United States is threatened. Equally inevitably, it will be harder now for the United States to rally international support for any action it wants to take. Not only are the Kurds divided, but Mr. Hussein has apparently also been careful not to send aircraft into the Erbil area in violation of the allied 'no flight' zone. The United States has never barred Iraqi military ground units from crossing the 36th parallel."[6]

Dole's problem was that he had spoken before he knew the particulars of the situation in Northern Iraq. On Sunday, he said "Saddam has been testing American leadership and finding it lacking." He ridiculed Vice President Gore for saying the situation needed to be studied before any action is taken, saying: "We don't need to analyze Saddam's actions. We need to condemn them."[7] Dole stopped short of urging military action, but Clinton did not, and when Dole had to comment on the bombing, he was not in any position to criticize it. His advisers, in this case led by Senator John McCain [R-AZ], goaded Dole into criticizing the President for not having taken more decisive action. Reading from his prepared script, Jack Kemp agreed.

At its source, however, the "mess in Iraq" had deeper sources. The United Nations did not resolve to create a "no-fly safety zone." It merely passed a resolution urging Saddam to stop repressing the Kurds. Baghdad was slaughtering the Kurds, who are citizens of Iraq because President Bush had urged the Kurds to rise up and overthrow Saddam and when they attempted to do just that, the Islamic equivalent of the Bay of Pigs ensued. The Bush administration's

---

6 R. W. Apple, Jr., "How to Slap Iraq?" *The New York Times*, September 2, 1996, p. A6.
7 Ibid.

implicit support of the uprising was a consolation prize to those who wanted General Schwartzkopf to slaughter Saddam's Republican Guard: "The best they can do now is argue that if only he had gone in, and we had taken over Iraq, the Kurds we incited to rebellion would not now be at each other's throats because the economy is in such terrible shape in the 'no-fly safety zone.'"[8]

Part of the reason for the Kurdish insurgency was that the economy in northern Iraq was in extraordinary disrepair. The Kurdish economy was in such bad shape because five years after the Gulf War, the United States continued to block the sale of Iraqi oil on the world market. In an ugly, vicious cycle, the U.S. had become mired in a power struggle with Saddam, angry over his stifling of a rebellion *the U.S.* incited, not because he had failed to meet the demands of the UN that he not acquire weapons of mass destruction. It first became obvious in 1994 that all such demands had been met by Baghdad, to the point of embarrassment at the UN and most of the governments of Europe. A 1990 War College report admits this readily.[9] Saddam Hussein had been "permanently demonized," to quote *The New York Times'* Mr. Apple,[10] when for years he had been our dictator of choice in the Iran-Iraq war. After the war, with Iraq bled white financially, Saddam Hussein became understandably irritated when the Emir of Kuwait, with a few hundred wives, was lolling in wealth by selling barrels of oil far above his agreed OPEC commitment, thus driving down the world oil price and making it virtually impossible for Iraq to pay its bills.

---

8 Ibid.

9 Michael Williams, Memo to Larry Hunter at Empower America, March 16, 1998. Williams cited the Army War College Report's most damning evidence with regard to claims of an Iraqi attack on the Kurds. State "does not specify what types of weapons were deployed, specific instances of use, nor does it produce corroborating evidence. No victims of these chemical attacks were discovered by international relief organizations in Turkey or Iraq. It is impossible to confirm the State Department's claim that gas was used in these instances."

10 R. W. Apple, Jr., "How to Slap Iraq?" *The New York Times*, September 2, 1996, p. A6.

It was [Bush's] Ambassador to Baghdad, April Glaspie, who told Saddam that the United States would not much mind if he exercised Iraq's claims on the oil fields of northern Kuwait. When Saddam grabbed the oil fields, nobody else in the neighborhood got excited, including Saudi Arabia, until President Bush decided to tell Saddam that April Glaspie didn't mean it, and he had to give up Iraq's claims.[11]

There obviously had been an unspoken agreement among the foreign policy gurus of both our political parties that Saddam would not be allowed to sell Iraqi oil on the world market, whether or not he complied with UN demands that he first meet certain conditions. This was the publicly avowed position of Richard Nixon, in his 1991 book on how to manage the post-war world. "While we should allow Iraq to purchase some humanitarian supplies, we must keep the sanctions in place as long as he remains in power."[12] Clearly the aim of our government was to cause such suffering in Iraq via the embargo that the people would rise up and kick Saddam out, or have him assassinated. As a parallel, this, of course, remains the written and spoken agreement between Democrats and Republicans on Cuba, the never ending hope that the people or the palace guard will take out Fidel Castro. It was this U.S. insistence on a continued economic squeeze on Iraq that led to the fighting among the Kurds in the summer of 1996. They were essentially fighting over the fast dwindling supply of calories. By this time, the UN estimated that 600,000 Iraqi children had died since August 1990 as a result of the sanctions, which brought widespread malnutrition and massive outbreaks of preventable diseases. An editorial in the September *Progressive*, published just before the September 3rd bombing, noted:

---

11 Jude Wanniski, "In Defense of Saddam Hussein," Polyconomics, Inc., Morristown, N.J., September 3, 1996.

12 Richard M. Nixon, *Seize the Moment* (New York, N.Y.: Simon & Schuster, 1991), p. 215.

What did these 600,000 Iraqi children do to deserve this fate? They were born inside the borders of a country that Washington chooses to strangle.

This May, after many entreaties by the international community, the United States finally signed on to a U.N. resolution allowing Iraq to sell $2 billion of oil every six months so it could purchase food, medicine, and other basic items. It's not a lot of money; in fact it would come to less than twenty five cents per Iraqi per day. But it would at least be something.

And something is now more than Washington wants to concede. In July, the Clinton Administration said that Iraq was planning to improperly use the proceeds of the oil sales. As a result, the exemption for the oil sale is now in question, and the people of Iraq continue to starve.

A few months ago on *60 Minutes*, Lesley Stahl interviewed Madeleine Albright, U.S. Ambassador to the U.N., about Washington's responsibility for the suffering in Iraq.

Stahl's question: "We have heard that a half million children have died. I mean, that is more children than died in Hiroshima. And, you know, is the price worth it?"

Ambassador Albright's response: "I think this is a very hard choice, but the price, we think, is worth it."[13]

It was in the days following the air strikes that it became clear President Clinton had pulled the trigger without consulting anyone in Congress or the Gulf allies! Even if Bob Dole had missed his chance to put Clinton on the spot at the time of the bombing, he now had a second chance to make an issue out of the fact that the

---

13 Editorial, "Back to Baghdad," *The Progressive*, September 1996, p. 10. It was the news that the long-awaited relief from oil sales was once again held up by the United States that triggered the power struggle among the two Kurdish factions in Northern Iraq.

President had acted wholly outside the Constitution. No other American President in history had ordered military action against another country without consulting anyone, except perhaps his campaign manager. William Jefferson Clinton had simply called Defense Secretary William Perry and said *'Bombs away!'*

Articles of impeachment would not have been out of line, except for the fact that there continued to be, as columnist Robert Novak put it on September 9, an "almost total absence of *political* opposition to Clinton's unilateral action." [emphasis added]

> Once-dovish Democrats dare not criticize their president, and hawkish Republicans demand even tougher military operations...Nobody who has the slightest knowledge of the real world labors under illusions that the U.S. attack has damaged Saddam Hussein or threatened his brutal reign. He is now stronger than ever...
>
> This is the dangerous climate of post-Cold War American policy. The national security and intelligence apparatus that fought the Soviet behemoth is still in place, and its attitude permeates the outlook of presidential candidate Bob Dole...
>
> So what did the missiles accomplish? Calamity for U.S. interests. Desert Storm's Arab-European coalition is shattered. Saddam is reestablished in northern Iraq. The United States stands exposed as a paper tiger for timidly undertaking an operation it should have avoided.
>
> Yet in the middle of a presidential election, Republicans hesitate to point out these harsh realities. Whatever criticism there is attacks Clinton for not hitting harder...The toughest criticism from top-ranking Republicans was Senate Majority Leader Trent Lott's complaint that he was not advised of the missile attacks in advance as required under the War Powers Act.

Sen. John McCain, a Dole adviser, was active on the Senate floor Thursday night pleading with colleagues not to vote against a resolution supporting the President's action. A 'no' vote, he said, would give the wrong idea to the world.[14]

A report from Amman, Jordan, by John Daniszewski of the *Los Angeles Times* made it clear Clinton had blundered: "The episode will significantly weaken the 5-year-old U.S. policy of isolating and containing the Iraqi dictator..."

In the wake of the attacks:

- Middle Eastern countries now speak more urgently about the need to reestablish diplomatic relations with Baghdad and bring Iraq back into the Arab fold, even with Hussein in control. An Arab consensus is forming that Iraq is no longer a military threat and that it has been humiliated by the United States.

- The Iraqi army's right to operate in Kurdish areas in the north of the country has been acknowledged and even welcomed by many of Iraq's neighbors and endorsed by countries like France, Russia and China.

- The governments of America's chief Arab allies – Saudi Arabia, Jordan and Egypt – already facing internal opposition, find themselves embarrassed and on the offensive.

In fact, and perhaps worst of all from a U.S. standpoint, the strikes have not accelerated the downfall of Hussein but rather appear to have increased his status and popularity amid rising anti-American emotions...Arab critics...saw it as being gratuitous, a purposeless display of superiority against an already beaten foe.[15]

---

14 Robert Novak, "Not a Victory," *The Washington Post*, September 9, 1996, p. A19.

15 John Daniszewski, "U.S. Strikes Give Baghdad a Boost Among Its Neighbors," *Los Angeles Times*, September 9, 1996, p. A1.

Against this backdrop, from every angle, it looked like a winning issue for Dole, if he had chosen to make an issue of Clinton's bumbling. Here there was a presidential "unibomber" willing to play soldier and order missiles fired thither and yon, as if he were king of the world. This Democratic President, who as a youth had dodged the draft, had done something no other right-wing Republican commander in chief had done. Just as in his treatment of the black vote in moving rightward on domestic issues, to say just slightly to the left of Gingrich, Clinton had left his left flank exposed by his gamble in bombing Iraq. In a political sense, it was a breathtaking gambit for Clinton. If Dole had challenged him on constitutional grounds or made an issue of the crass political nature of his risky military adventure, Clinton would have suffered in many ways. If Dole had forced the electorate to focus on what Clinton had done, the entire GOP establishment would have had to get behind him and denounce the President for recklessness. The President's Democratic faithful, quietly horrified at what he had done, but willing to bite their tongues in order to win in November, would have had to confront a Dole suddenly on the high ground and positioned *to the left* of the President – arguing diplomacy instead of missiles. Remember, at this time Dole trailed Clinton by 20 points or more in the polls because he was so far behind with women.

Throughout this period, I had been communicating almost daily with Kemp about the opening the campaign had. He and his campaign staff agreed, but advised they had to wait a bit, "until the smoke cleared." The Dole campaign was being driven on this issue by Senator McCain, and Dole could not bring himself to shift gears to a discussion of the proprieties involved. After his first statement of support, Kemp did begin criticizing the bombing as "precipitous," but that was as far as he thought he could go. As a result, that mild, elliptical criticism of Clinton foreign policy had no impact on the campaign. As long as Dole himself would not become engaged, the political media were not interested in the background grumblings of Kemp and Senator Lott.

Kemp hoped he would be able to give a speech on foreign policy and on September 8, I suggested he deal with Iraq as a way of discussing America's role in the new unipolar world.

> When the President takes military action, there is no choice by political leaders of all parties but to rally to his action. But there is a great unease throughout our country about a President who can order the bombing of a sovereign nation without consulting a single member of Congress or any political leader anywhere on earth. I would not go so far as to say, as Ross Perot has, that our President dropped these bombs in order to get a bump in the polls. But it was *precipitous* – an action ordered to distract our attention from the failures of our foreign policy in this part of the world.
>
> We know President Clinton did not order the bombing of Switzerland or Sweden. We also know Saddam Hussein is not Santa Claus. He is not a pleasant fellow. But he is the head of state of a sovereign nation-state. It is not up to us to say he is not the legitimate leader of the Iraqi people. If we could get Iraq's neighbors to petition us to get rid of him, and if we could get the great majority of the international community to agree that he must be removed from power, then we could treat him as a common criminal.
>
> But this is not the case. Quite the contrary, we find that none of Saddam's neighbors looked upon our precipitous bombing of Iraq without deep concern that he had not acted wisely – not Saudi Arabia, not Jordan, not Egypt. And of the rest of the world, only Great Britain spoke up with support, in the same spirit that Bob Dole and I spoke up – knowing we had little other choice. Our President and

Commander in Chief had committed our armed forces to military action and we had to salute.[16]

Except for the column by Robert Novak and a critique of Clinton's *"ad hoc"* air strikes by Michael Kelly of *The New Yorker*,[17] there were no complaints from the mainstream press. Had the *Times* or *The Washington Post* even raised an eyebrow, Dole might have found a way to join the issue, perhaps with a nudge from Kemp. But if *The Wall Street Journal* and the rest of the conservative press were content to only criticize Clinton for not dropping big enough bombs, the President's supporters in the press were happy enough to let this sleeping dog lie. President Clinton's gamble had paid off in a big way. He got to fire a few missiles at a demonized Saddam and the voters were left with the impression that if Dole were President, he would have dropped a lot more bombs.

The denouement of this element of the campaign came in Kemp's debate with Vice President Al Gore on October 9, when he took a direct shot at Clinton's Iraqi adventure. The Kemp phrase that lingered in the minds of those Republicans who Colin Powell refers to as "bombers," was directed at the President: "Don't bomb before breakfast!" More than anything else he did or did not do in the campaign, this one comment brought down the wrath of the Republican Cold Warriors, "the bombers." In the lead was George

---

16 Jude Wanniski, Memo to Jack Kemp, September 8, 1996. Kemp almost never read from a prepared text, but he was an insatiable consumer of ideas and talking points. I don't know how much of the material I sent him during the campaign he used in the more than one hundred speeches he delivered between August and November. Only an occasional comment made it into the national press. In the last three weeks of the campaign, scarcely a word from Kemp made it into print.

17 Michael Kelly, "Iraq Ad Hoc," *The New Yorker*, September 16, 1996, p. 7. Kelly's wry critique was unusual in that it came from a publication associated with dovish views on foreign policy: "It is a good thing to hit Saddam Hussein whenever an opportunity presents itself (and it is certainly a satisfying thing, and it is even more certainly a thing popular with the voters), but the fact is that the interests of no American friends or allies were threatened by Saddam's campaign to seize the city of Erbil from the forces of the Patriotic Union of Kurdistan."

Foreign Policy: Bombs Before Breakfast

Will, whose Sunday column in *The Washington Post*, two days before the election, was dedicated to dumping on Kemp's performance in the campaign: "Kemp attacked Clinton's foreign policy from the left ('Don't bomb before breakfast'), by criticizing Clinton for asserting American power without seeking the permission of allies. Republicans should apologize to the country for proposing to put Kemp near the presidency."[18] In the column, Will noted that Kemp was "evidently prompted by a crackpot adviser (Jude Wanniski)" for the Farrakhan initiative and the bombing before breakfast remark. In a November 16 letter to the *Post*, I said: "Will makes a serious error when he accuses Kemp of criticizing Bill Clinton 'for asserting American power without seeking the permission of allies.' To be sure, Kemp thought it would have been seemly if the president had asked the opinion of America's coalition allies in the Persian Gulf. His central complaint, though, was that Clinton did not consult with a single member of the 104th Congress before pulling the trigger on Iraq."

Historians looking back on the 1996 presidential contest will have to marvel at what President Clinton had gotten away with. Here was the Republican Majority Leader of the United States Senate, Trent Lott of Mississippi, himself no dove, criticizing a President who is running for re-election for having violated the War Powers Act – an impeachable offense – and the matter is dropped just like that.

Dropped, but not forgotten. Months after the election, *The New York Times Magazine* devoted its cover story to the most powerful man in the 105th Congress, Trent Lott. It is a largely adulatory profile of Lott by Richard Berke, a *Times* political writer. At one point, Berke notes that Clinton might "find Lott to be less deferential than Dole if a foreign policy crisis erupts. 'Bob Dole was a person who had a reverence for the office of the Presidency,' [Senator] McCain says. 'He supported the constitutional authority of the President as Commander in Chief. That's an area where we may have trouble.

---

18 George F. Will, "Thunder But No Rain," *The Washington Post*, November 3, 1996, p. C7.

Suppose another Bosnia arises? Lott just doesn't have the broad years of experience that Bob Dole has.'"[19]

Oddly enough, if Dole had been President, there is nobody who knows him who believes he would have acted as recklessly as Clinton in skirting the War Powers Act by not consulting Congress. As a former member of and leader in the Senate, surely he would have done so. Still, his apparent passivity on this issue left voters no choice but to assume he would have joined McCain and the opinion leaders who insisted Clinton should have acted more vigorously in the use of force. In the course of the campaign, Dole had gone as far as to suggest he would ask Colin Powell to be his Secretary of State. The diplomatic former NATO ambassador Robert Ellsworth, one of Dole's closest friends, was certainly no "bomber." But Ellsworth was reluctant to insert his opinion into the campaign unless he was asked and Ellsworth was never asked. The Kemp team could not understand why, but two of the most devout "bombers" in Washington – Richard Perle and Paul Wolfowitz[20] – had become part of the inner circle of the Dole campaign. Was it their fault that their national security views kept Dole to the right of Clinton, when there was no reason for him to be there? Not at all. With his "broad years of experience," Dole went into the most important campaign of his life without really thinking about foreign policy.

---

19 Richard L. Berke, "Trent Lott and His Fierce Freshmen," *The New York Times Magazine*, February 2, 1997, p. 48.

20 Perle and Wolfowitz, protégés of the late nuclear strategist Albert Wohlstetter, were the two most aggressive members of the Pentagon intellectuals in the Reagan administration.

CHAPTER TEN

A Winning Issue, by Executive Order

F rom the very beginning of President Clinton's campaign for re-election, the only issue that seemed possible to work for a Republican challenger was economic growth. This is the issue that enabled Ronald Reagan to deny Jimmy Carter a second term, and it was the only issue that could dislodge Bill Clinton. The American electorate had come out of 50 years of Cold War with a pile of problems that could only be solved by rapid, non-inflationary economic growth. The U.S. economy had been going backwards since 1967, when the first signs of the coming monetary inflation began and interest rates began to creep up. President Nixon made matters worse in 1969, by deferring his campaign promise to eliminate LBJ's Vietnam war tax and by increasing the tax on capital gains.[1] Capital formation then began a long decline as Presidents Nixon and Carter tried to fix the economy by a series of tax increases and currency devaluations that only made matters worse. With less capital forming, labor had to work harder to make ends meet. This meant a steady decline in the standard of living for the majority of Americans, from the bottom up. Reagan reversed the process. With his tax cuts and the accompanying currency appreciation, the U.S. economy grew by

---

1 After his inauguration in 1969, Nixon was persuaded to postpone his promise to eliminate the 10% income surtax by his Council of Economic Advisers, who believed it should remain in place in order to collect more revenues. Herbert Stein, who later became chairman of the CEA, was also an opponent of the lower capital gains tax and helped persuade Nixon it could be raised. When the economy went into a serious contraction, Stein was among those who persuaded Nixon it was caused by the Federal Reserve's tight money policy. This put Nixon on track to close the gold window in 1971, to permit a devaluation of the dollar that was supposed to expand the economy.

a third, in real terms, during his eight years.[2] When George Bush broke his "read my lips" pledge, he pushed the economy and real wages back into contraction. The voters would not accept his apologies.

President Clinton was a marginal improvement over the previous Democrat in the White House, Jimmy Carter, largely because he learned from Carter's mistakes. In one way, he was superior to President Bush, whose Treasury Secretary Nick Brady believed in the formula that got Jimmy Carter into trouble. Brady believed that raising taxes to balance the budget would cause interest rates to fall and the economy to grow. When interest rates did not fall with this prescription, Brady kept up a steady criticism of the Federal Reserve for not simply lowering interest rates. The way the international market for U.S. securities works, Treasury's agitation for easier money only served to keep investors skittish about holding U.S. government bonds, which thus had the effect of keeping rates higher than they would have been if Brady had simply kept his mouth shut. By the end of the Bush administration, Brady and Fed Chairman Alan Greenspan were barely on speaking terms.

In his first two years, President Clinton was scarcely better than President Bush on fiscal policy. He not only raised tax rates on "the rich" in his first year, 1993, but also made the effective date of the increase retroactive, prior to a point where he was still promising a middle-class tax cut. He did so without a single Republican vote. On monetary policy, on the other hand, the Clinton administration consistently supported Greenspan, except for one small slip of the tongue from Treasury Secretary Lloyd Bentsen at a 1993 National Press Club speech. When the financial markets trembled at this ghost of Nick Brady, there were no further comments from Bentsen or his successor, Bob Rubin, about the conduct of monetary or

---

2 Measured against the price of gold, the stock market climbed 600 percent in Reagan's two terms, having fallen 60 percent in the Nixon-Carter years. In other words, if the economy doubles in dollar terms, but the dollar price of gold doubles at the same time, the economy has not really moved at all.

exchange-rate policy, at least not without the blessing of Greenspan. Clinton "did a rather poor job of trying to interpret the 'mandate' given him by only 43 percent of the vote in a three-way race with George Bush and Ross Perot. Yet he didn't do much damage. The Republican minority was adroit enough to block his health-care initiatives. And the President wisely stayed on the good side of Fed Chairman Alan Greenspan, which counts for a lot."[3]

President Clinton would have a better second term than his first, which is what the financial markets seemed to be saying at the time. "The President has run up the learning curve and has a seasoned team in place...He clearly has earned the respect of his global counterparts – who are so far grateful that he has effectively brought order to Bosnia, their own backyard, but that he also has done nothing to precipitate a global recession."[4] Greenspan is firmly in place at the Fed, and although the GOP might lose the House in November, the GOP almost certainly would remain in control of the Senate.

Senator Dole was fighting an uphill battle. "Women and minorities are *afraid of Bob Dole* because they see in him a Cold Warrior who wants to balance the budget – *which is what he is, for goodness sakes.*" The people at the bottom of the socio-economic ladder had just experienced a 30-year decline in real wages that paralleled the sacrifices of the Cold War. They *"have to be frightened* by a candidate who: 1) pledges to expand military outlays in order to confront the hostile world he envisions; 2) threatens to enlarge NATO in order to isolate the Russians as a means of stoking that hostility; and 3) vows to balance the budget no matter what it takes."[5]

Getting over this fear was a tall order. It at least seemed possible with his choice of Kemp as Vice President on August 9. Dole could not close the gap with policy speeches, advertising or a woman as

---

3 Jude Wanniski, "In Defense of the President," Polyconomics, Inc., Morristown, N.J., July 2, 1996.

4 Ibid.

5 Ibid.

his running mate. It would take substantive action, and Kemp was a good first step. With Dick Morris at Clinton's elbow as he played this ultimate game in political chess, the President had put Dole in check with his sophisticated strategies, but it was not yet checkmate. Columnist Bob Novak knew Morris fairly well and understood what his strategy was all about – shadowing the GOP while pushing them further to the right. He could not think of a way the Republicans could beat it. *If the President moved further to the right to shadow the GOP, he would always seem more centrist.*[6] The only possible out for Dole was with the promise of executive orders. If the Republican candidate would pledge to sign executive orders on tax and monetary policy – on the first day of his presidency – he could overleap Clinton's shadow strategy. In other words, *the Republicans should promise to do things that Clinton would be unable to copy and would probably be tempted to attack.*

These were the same executive orders mentioned in Chapter Four, which Kemp had written about in his June 18 op-ed essay in *The Wall Street Journal.* The final version was the work of Kemp and his chief economist at Empower America, Larry Hunter. Written as "A Bipartisan Economic Agenda,"[7] it got zero attention, because Kemp was seen to be totally outside any role in the campaign. Yet it was among the best political documents produced in the course of the year. The *Journal* ran it across the top of its editorial page:

> It is not that deficits don't matter, they emphatically do – in the same way that a high fever matters. Both are symptoms of much deeper maladies. In the case of deficits, the real malady is the anemic rate of growth in the economy and a political system that has lost the ability to set national priorities. It is not enough to say that government

---

6 A long lunch at the Army-Navy Club in Washington to discuss strategy with Novak, himself a brilliant political chess kibitzer, revealed all this.

7 Jack F. Kemp, "A Bipartisan Economic Agenda," *The Wall Street Journal,* June 18, 1996, p. A22.

is too big and that it overspends. The problem is that the economy isn't growing fast enough to accommodate the level of spending produced through the democratic process....[8]

At the time his op-ed appeared, Kemp believed that Clinton almost certainly would be re-elected, barring a smoking gun in one of the many White House scandals that had been emerging without result. Hence, his argument would be on behalf of a bipartisan agenda. In the essay, Kemp referred back to a *Journal* op-ed piece that appeared two months earlier, on April 11, that took up almost the entire op-ed space of the page. Simply entitled "Recipe for Growth," it was by Felix Rohatyn of the New York investment bank of Lazard Freres, the most prominent Democrat on Wall Street and the man credited with saving New York City from bankruptcy in 1976. The *Journal* had given Rohatyn so much space because his essay was something of an ideological confession of error from one of the most prominent Democrats of our time. It was seen in political circles as an extremely important political statement, one that pushed in the direction that I thought Clinton would like to take as a "New Democrat."

The genesis of the article was a happenstance airplane conversation Rohatyn had earlier in the year with Ted Forstmann, who had backed Kemp in his 1988 race and was now backing Dole. Both had decried the mindset that occupied the business and political establishments of both parties, which held that the economy could not grow faster than $2^{1}/_{2}$ percent annually without reigniting inflation. The two men agreed to co-author an essay which they would submit to the *Journal*. Forstmann produced a draft, but as they quickly saw how difficult it would be to write a piece that would satisfy both of them, Rohatyn decided to do something different. If history would record the political world in the United States pivoting on its axis during these years, the Rohatyn manifesto would be the place to focus.

---

8 Ibid.

He began by acknowledging that as a traditional Democrat he always believed that fairness required a fairly steeply graduated income tax – and when combined with lower deficits would guarantee adequate growth and a fair distribution of wealth. The experience of the last two decades, with the advent of the global economy, had very much shaken that view: "Fairness does not require the redistribution of wealth; it requires the creation of wealth, geared to an economy that can provide employment for everyone willing and able to work, and the opportunity for a consistently higher standard-of-living for those employed."[9]

Rohatyn discouraged the idea that there could soon be a reduction in the differential in current levels of income and wealth, saying they are likely to increase in the near future as the requirements for skills and education increase. Yes, the world is not fair, he said, but we must "make it better for those in the middle as well as those at the lower end of the economic scale." Here is the key: "*Enough growth that, even if initially the lower end does not gain as rapidly as the upper, it can improve its absolute standard of living, and begin a process of closing the gap.*" How do we get there? "[It] requires a tax system that promotes growth as its main objective. It must encourage higher investment and savings. That is not the case today. Today's tax system aims at a concept of fairness dictated by distribution tables. That may not be the best test..."[10]

Here, Rohatyn directly confronted the traditional Democratic argument that lower tax rates on capital represented "trickle-down" economics: "Lowering taxes on capital would at first blush seem to help the already wealthy, current holders of capital. But whatever its effect on the distribution tables, it could unleash powerful capital flows, both domestic and foreign, that would lower interest rates significantly and make investment in the U.S. even more competitive

---

9 Felix G. Rohatyn, "Recipe for Growth," *The Wall Street Journal*, April 11, 1996, p. A16.
10 Ibid.

than it is today...If the Democrats can redefine their concept of fairness, Republicans, on the other hand, may have to abandon their view of passive government."[11]

In referring back favorably to the op-ed, Kemp noted Rohatyn "had suggested that the first step toward reviving robust economic growth is to forge an entente between the parties, centered on an agreement that economic growth is our nation's highest and first priority. I agree. Wouldn't it be wonderful if both parties were debating how to double the rate of economic growth rather than seeing who can get the most tax credits and targeted tax cuts into the existing Internal Revenue Code?" Kemp cited Rohatyn's appeal to Democrats, to shift their focus to growing the economy so that the "have nots have more."[12]

He then asked Republicans to "make it possible for Democrats to give up their quest for redistribution of income and wealth by our acceptance of an appropriate role for government in financing those public goods and services necessary to secure a social safety net below which no American would be allowed to fall." He noted that the huge government bureaucracy in place was created over the last 60 years with good intentions, but with a redistributionist philosophy that led to counterproductive results. "In the face of this reality, we Republicans make a serious mistake when we try to economize first on social programs. It allows us to be characterized as putting the 'cart' of fiscal austerity before the 'horse' of rapid economic growth."[13]

After a discussion of the need to replace the existing tax structure instead of patching it up one more time, Kemp brought up the executive orders as a "down payment." First, he said the President should instruct the Treasury secretary to index against inflation the treatment of capital gains, retroactively as well as prospectively. "This

---

11 Ibid.
12 Jack F. Kemp, "A Bipartisan Economic Agenda," *The Wall Street Journal*, June 18, 1996, p. A22.
13 Ibid.

action would instantly remove the tax liabilities on several trillion dollars worth of capital assets – mostly farm and real property but also including considerable financial assets held long term – that are purely the result of inflation and are not real capital gains at all. While there remains a partisan dispute over the treatment of genuine capital gains, there has been broad bipartisan agreement that inflated gains should not be taxed."[14]

Secondly, he said the new president should instruct the Treasury secretary to stabilize the dollar value of the nation's gold reserves, within a $30 band, as a critical first step toward restoring sound money to America. "This action would reinstate the dollar-gold link that was broken in 1971, which led to the most severe run of inflation in our nation's history...Restoring the dollar-gold link is the surest proven method of taking the risk out of the dollar and all other government debt...For every percentage point that interest rates fall, the federal government would save more than $50 billion a year in interest outlays on its current $5.1 trillion national debt. That means we could save $1 trillion in debt-service costs during the next decade by refinancing the national debt at the much lower interest rates that would result when the risk of inflation was removed from the dollar."[15]

These lower interest rates – eventually as low as 3 percent on 30-year bonds and 4 percent on 30-year mortgages – also would foster a dramatic increase in private-sector capital formation, he argued. "Economists in both parties, supply-siders and demand-siders alike, agree that the living standards of wage earners can only rise with the kind of productivity increases that accompany rapid capital formation and lower long-term interest rates."[16]

---

14 Ibid.

15 Ibid.

16 Ibid. The idea of an executive order indexing capital gains was first proposed by Paul Craig Roberts in a *Washington Times* column in January 1992. The Bush administration considered doing it during the 1992 campaign, but decided not to when a Justice Department lawyer raised a minor technical objection.

A Winning Issue, by Executive Order

When the Rohatyn article appeared on April 11, Kemp called him and discussed the idea of having a joint day-long conference on economic growth. Rohatyn was amenable to the idea, but the discussions ended when the White House got wind of it and urged Rohatyn to postpone it until late in the year. Larry Hunter told me he understood the concern at the White House was that Kemp might use the conference to help the Dole campaign. In any case, the matter was dropped, but I told Kemp I thought Rohatyn's statement represented a sea change in Democratic intellectual circles, that Rohatyn would not have written the piece if he didn't know it was already ripe within the Democratic establishment. After more than 60 years of tax-the-rich, Robin Hood rhetoric, the Democratic center-of-gravity had shifted. In this I could see the beginnings of a realignment of the parties, which would give Republicans dominance as long as they accepted the Rohatyn formula.

The idea of using an executive order to link the dollar-gold rate was one most supply-siders had been familiar with since Columbia University Professor Robert Mundell first suggested it in September 1981, when the plunging gold price was driving the U.S. economy into its worst monetary deflation since the 1870s. There was never any hope that Dole would allow it to be brought into his campaign, although he was familiar with the arguments. Two of his closest friends in politics were sympathetic to the idea, former Fed Governor Wayne Angell, a Kansan with close ties to Dole, and Senator Robert Bennett of Utah, Dole's point man on the health-care issue. As good as the idea may be, though, the political operatives around Dole would have rebelled at anything to do with "a gold standard," and nobody was about to try. The capital-gains tax, on the other hand, had over the years come to the top of the GOP agenda. In a 1995 "Meet the Press" interview, when Tim Russert asked Dole what the first thing he would do as President, he said he would cut the capital gains tax. Throughout the fall campaign, Dole consistently listed a lower capital gains rate as one of the prime goals of his administration, as did Kemp. Fed Chairman Alan Greenspan, the arbiter of budget orthodoxy in the GOP, had in recent years made his position known that he favored elimination of the capgains tax, on the grounds that it was a direct tax on the national standard of living and would do more harm than good at any rate, even 1 percent.

President Clinton did not contest the issue with any vehemence, preferring to list an exemption on capital gains taxation for the sale of the family homestead. In 1992, Clinton had campaigned in Silicon Valley and on Wall Street with whispered assurances that he favored a cut in the capital gains tax. The idea of having Dole pledge to wipe out all gains that had accrued to American farmers, businessmen and homeowners through an executive order was something that could force the issue center stage in the campaign. It was foremost in my mind at the San Diego convention in August, and in every encounter I had with the Dole political people, I made the argument that Dole-Kemp could win California with this single campaign issue. The only interested party was Charlie Black, who had been Kemp's campaign manager in 1988 and was now a consultant to Dole. But it always seemed too complicated to political operatives who preferred the simplicity of a 15 percent tax cut, which we warned would not sell as long as the Democrats could argue it would be paid for by cutting Medicare benefits.

The idea was a big one because it involved *seven trillion dollars.* I even wrote out the number so they would grasp its immensity: $7,000,000,000,000. In other words, seven thousand billion dollars. This is based on the idea that since the United States left the gold standard by Nixon's executive order in 1971, the inflation of the price tag of the whole country had gone up tenfold. The country's net worth in 1996 was roughly $30 trillion – lock, stock and barrel. Of that, $8 trillion represents the capital gain of all farms, mines, mills, small businesses and homes. Of the $8 trillion, $7 trillion is pure inflation, and should not be taxed at all. The U.S. government is sitting in wait for the owners of all these assets to be forced to sell, and pay a capgains tax of 28 percent on the one-eighth that is real and the seven-eighths that is inflation. By the stroke of a pen, the President, be he Clinton or Dole, could wipe out the tax liabilities on that $7 trillion – a tax cut of almost $2 trillion. Because California represents between one-sixth and one-seventh of the capital assets of the whole United States, the stroke of that presidential pen would lift at least $300 billion in tax liabilities from the backs of Californians.

If Dole promised he would sign such an order on Day One as President, and his campaign backed him up with television commercials making the pledge, he would have a realistic chance of winning California and the election itself. He could even write out the executive order and wave it over his head in campaign speeches. It would be a way of overcoming the cynicism of voters throughout America whose most recent experience with Republicans was George Bush breaking his "read my lips" pledge and Newt Gingrich and Bob Dole shutting down the government. In 1988, Bush had campaigned on a promise to cut the capital gains tax to 15 percent, from 28 percent, and never delivered. In his Contract With America, Gingrich pledged to cut the capital gains tax to 15 percent, from 28 percent, and never delivered. Dole's promise to deliver a 15 percent income-tax cut when he could barely defend it against the ridicule of the Clinton campaign was a worthless issue, one that Kemp was stuck with.

For Dole to promise an executive order wiping out $2 trillion in tax liabilities was not only credible. It also could not be challenged seriously by the President. Clinton could never oppose lifting an unjust and immoral tax burden from the backs of farmers, small businessmen and homeowners, and Democratic economists had always acknowledged that inflated gains should not be taxed. It was "a pat hand." Indeed, the only strenuous GOP arguments why Dole should not campaign on this issue was that Clinton would steal the idea, do it *immediately*, and reap the political benefits himself. Perhaps he would have, but as President, Clinton would have to subject the idea to such a vetting process that it couldn't done prior to the election. After Clinton's re-election, Kemp asked for a meeting with the President to urge him to sign such an executive order. The meeting took place on July 15, 1997, with Vice President Al Gore and Treasury Secretary Bob Rubin present. Rubin rejected the idea on several technical grounds that Kemp assumed would be made. Still, he wanted it on the record that if the President wanted to do this for his personal legacy, Kemp would make it his business to rally Republican support.

By asking the *electorate* for a mandate, Dole would override the technical complaints of the Treasury bureaucrats. The promise would give Dole a cutting-edge idea that he could actually deliver on his first day in office. The problem was that nobody in the Dole campaign was interested in adding it to their daily chores. The new media team of Paul Manafort and Rick Davis and the pollster, Tony Fabrizio, had been given almost total artistic and strategic license by campaign manager Scott Reed. They were not interested in new ideas from the Kemp team, and although Reed came to take a greater interest in the executive-order idea, he could never get past the inner circle that supposedly worked for him. Having no political experience himself at this level, Reed found himself being intimidated by the team's arrogance and credentials.

The only reason the idea kept going is that Ted Forstmann was pushing it inside with campaign with Scott Reed. It was Forstmann who had persuaded many, including Kemp, that the retroactive indexation of capital gains would do far more for the economy than simply cutting the tax rate itself. I'd assumed Forstmann had enough clout with Dole and Don Rumsfeld, the National Campaign Chairman, to get it done. Dole himself was impressed by Forstmann, having heard of his prodigious financial feats, his political philanthropies and his money-raising powers. One would think that with this kind of "juice" inside the campaign, Forstmann could move the issue along fairly quickly. It took two months of wrangling, though, before Kemp finally got the green light, on October 14, three weeks before the election:

> At an Anaheim meeting today of the California League of Cities, Jack Kemp is scheduled to announce a decision by Bob Dole to promise that on the first day of his presidency, he will issue an executive order that will instruct the Treasury Department to index capital gains for tax purposes, retroactively and prospectively. It is a major victory for Kemp, who wrote about the idea in a June 18 *Wall Street Journal* op-ed piece, several weeks before Dole chose him as his running mate. Kemp and his economic advisors at Empower America have been working with the Dole team since the San Diego convention on the feasibility of the idea. The last hurdles were cleared when Dole's concerns about the constitutional propriety of sidestepping the Congress [were] resolved through a letter from Charles Cooper, a Washington lawyer who served as Assistant Attorney General in the Reagan Administration...Cooper headed a legal team that attempted to persuade President Bush to issue such an executive order in 1992, when it became clear that Bush's campaign promise of 1988 to index capital gains by statute was not going to be achieved in a Democratic Congress...The California Field Poll shows Clinton's 20-point lead over Dole having narrowed to 10 points. The argument that Californians would have a tremendous stake in a Dole presidency as a result of the promise of this executive order may have contributed to the decision to move forward now. The news of the Kemp speech should be on the wires this afternoon.[17]

---

17 Jude Wanniski, "Breakthrough on Indexing Capgains," Polyconomics, Inc., Morristown, N.J., October 14, 1996.

A Winning Issue, by Executive Order

It wasn't on the wires that afternoon. Kemp did speak to more than 2,500 California mayors and city officials in Anaheim, departing from his prepared text to explain the decision. He received an ovation, with much of the audience cheering on their feet. "They seemed to understand immediately what it would mean to them and their communities," he said. He flew on to Palm Springs and Las Vegas that day, repeating the statement, with similar responses. *Yet there was not a word on the wires.* No reporter seemed to comprehend its importance. "Alas, the political reporters on Kemp's campaign plane have treated the idea as if it were economic boilerplate...The financial writers at least promise to look into the matter if Dole mentions it tonight in the debate."[18]

The second of the two Clinton-Dole debates was in San Diego that night. Kemp told me that Dole had been prepped to bring up the promise in the course of the debate and was willing to do so. A clear, declarative statement that he would sign the executive order soon after the inauguration is all that was needed. It was not to be. The debate format was not conducive to a discussion of the issue as the questions directed at the candidates came from a group of citizens instead of journalists. Near the end of the debate Dole seemed to remember what he had been prepped to do and mentioned the $7 trillion number in the same sentence as the capital gains tax. It was out of context, though, and a flustered Dole muttered aloud that there should be another debate just to discuss the economy. Of course, there never was another debate.

The issue was nearly dead, but Forstmann took one more shot, writing about it in *The Wall Street Journal.* It was the first mention of the idea in the nation's leading financial publication. Forstmann began: "On Oct. 14, Jack Kemp told 2,500 mayors and officials at a California League of Cities convention in Anaheim that as president

---

18 Jude Wanniski, "Notes on Campaign '96 V," Polyconomics, Inc., Morristown, N.J., October 16, 1996.

Bob Dole would sign an executive order instructing the Treasury Department to index capital gains to inflation for tax purposes. I was alarmed that political reporters present did not report the news; this was surely because they did not understand this announcement's great importance."[19]

As late as it came, the Forstmann piece was enough to keep the idea on life support. In the last two weeks of the campaign, if Dole could recover from his failure to bring up the idea in San Diego, Republican governors were now awakened. Michigan's Governor John Engler said he would do what he could to rally the other governors behind Kemp's idea, but that it wouldn't go anywhere unless Dole himself made a big deal out of it. I told Engler I would call some other governors myself. I faxed the Forstmann piece to Dr. Philip Romero, California Governor's Pete Wilson's chief economist in Sacramento, who called to say it was the first he heard about it – even though it had surfaced in his own state. He told me he thought it was a wonderful idea, that he would discuss it immediately with Governor Wilson, and recommend he give Dole support on it. "It's not going to do any good in winning the election," said Romero, who said he thought Dole was too far behind to catch up with anything new at that late date. "It's something that should be done and maybe we can get Clinton to do it next year."

It occurred to me that of all the Republican governors, the one who most understood the importance of a low capital gains tax was Tommy Thompson of Wisconsin. At the same time that taxes were being raised by governors such as Republican Wilson in California and Democrat James Florio in New Jersey, on top of the Bush tax increase of 1990, Thompson had fought through his Democratic legislature a cut in the capital gains tax. California and New Jersey quickly went into economic decline and Wisconsin surged ahead,

---

19 Theodore J. Forstmann, "Indexing Capital Gains – A Very Big Deal," *The Wall Street Journal*, October 22, 1996, p. A23.

adding 86,000 new manufacturing jobs in the past decade.[20] On October 24, I called the governor, who I had met just once, and faxed him a memo and the Forstmann article. He called me at home that evening. "This is a great idea," he said. "What do you want me to do?" I told him the best thing he could do would be to contact Dole himself to fire him up. He said he doubted he could get through to Dole because of a dustup between them a few weeks earlier. Thompson had been quoted in *The New York Times* making a disparaging comment about the Dole campaign, for which he then apologized in a letter to Dole. He said he would try, however, and he did.

Earlier in the campaign, I'd been talking to Kemp only two or three times a week, instead conveying messages through his staff aides or by my faxes to whatever hotel he would be at that night. In these last three weeks of the campaign, he began calling me from the road every day, sometimes two or three times, to discuss the options still open. "This race is so *winnable*, I can *taste* it," he said in one call that week, when he asked if Thompson had made the call to Dole. I assured him that Thompson understood that the race really could close with an unexpected upset. In my October 24 memo to Thompson, I had noted: "The race may seem over, but it is not. The Reuters-Zogby poll shows the ticket closing to 4 points in the West and in single digits in California. On Saturday, Dole will have a radio address that I believe will be the second most important thing he will have done in this otherwise miserable campaign. As Kellyanne Fitzpatrick, a GOP pollster, indicates on the *WSJ* editorial page today, there remains an enormous undecided vote..."

In the end, there was total frustration, as the candidate himself simply refused to budge. On Monday November 4, election eve, Bob Novak wrote a pre-post-mortem in his syndicated column, in which he cited the frustration with Dole on this specific issue. Novak said

---

20 Tommy Thompson, *Power to the People* (New York, N.Y.: HarperCollins, 1996), p. 158.

Dole, a "warrior to the end," did not lack the will to win, but a strategy: "What was lacking was demonstrated to me shortly after Dole announced his resignation last spring, when I lunched with one of the candidate's oldest, closest advisers. He made it clear that there was little chance that Dole would come up with even a modified flat tax or any radical tax reform. Instead he would propose an unadorned tax cut, which turned out to be the 15 percent reduction...Kemp was selected not only to transform the San Diego convention from a wake into a celebration but also to spread the ticket's appeal...[He] knew that the humdrum tax cut would generate no prairie fire..."[21]

What happened? Said Novak: "Kemp's announcement was not followed by confirmation by Dole himself, resulting in extraordinary news media silence. Could it be that Kemp was misrepresenting Dole? No, I was assured by a senior Dole campaign official, the presidential candidate was fully on board. So why did he not talk about it? 'We thought this was something more appropriate for Jack to handle,' the official told me. So, while Dole doggedly sold the 15 percent tax plan that voters doubt can ever be enacted, he ignored a chance to promise something he could accomplish with one stroke of the pen."[22]

For whatever reason, Dole did not jump on the horse Kemp had saddled for him. It could not have been for technical or legal reasons, for the campaign high command had allowed Kemp to ride the horse himself. There was plenty of documentation that it could

---

21 Robert Novak, "The Man Who Didn't Dare," *The Washington Post*, November 4, 1996, p. A19.

22 Ibid. In the column, Novak also mentioned Kemp's "audacious sally" in trying to bring the black vote to the ticket via Louis Farrakhan: "Addressing Jewish leaders, Kemp... called on the Nation of Islam leader to renounce antisemitism. Farrakhan did just that in early October, asserting: 'I denounce antisemitism in all its forms.' Kemp hailed this as a 'positive statement,' but Dole's staff was horrified, and Dole himself was silent. Farrakhan is the one major black leader willing to try to lead African Americans off the Democratic plantation, and close associates signaled he was eager to do so if Dole was interested. Dole was not."

be done. Dole also knew the issue and knew the people who would benefit most from such an executive order would be his Kansas farmers, so it was not out of fear that if he brought it up, he could not explain it.

Naturally, there's no guarantee that if Dole had actually campaigned on the executive-order promises that he would have done better than he did. The people he had entrusted with the paid advertising side of the campaign would have had to get behind it instead of throwing tens of millions of dollars away on negative TV spots. They clearly thought Kemp was a burden to them and that I was a nuisance. I thought again and again, doesn't Dole realize he can't win unless he gives the electorate *reasons to vote for him*? Didn't he see he had to *neutralize the President's promise to protect them from Newt Gingrich*? Okay, they don't like the executive orders. There was still one more idea we thought could turn the tide and win. Dole could tell the voters what kind of President he would be.

CHAPTER ELEVEN

Trust Me

D ole's last shot at winning the confidence of an electorate that clearly did not trust him in combination with Newt Gingrich and a GOP Congress was to persuade the voters that he could be trusted. Once again, the germ of an idea came from Ted Forstmann, who believed Dole's greatest strength as a political leader was that he always kept his word. Dole's personal integrity was the foundation upon which his career as a legislative leader was built. Jack Germond, *The Baltimore Sun's* liberal curmudgeon, observed on one of his talk show appearances that if a secret ballot were to be held in the U.S. Senate between Dole and Clinton, Dole would win 75 of the 100 votes. In a telephone conversation with Scott Reed, Forstmann argued that Dole's people were not marketing this Dole attribute that had not been challenged by the opposition, because this is one sure thing you could say about Dole, the heart of his success as a legislative leader. At the same time, there were very few Americans who had watched President Clinton during his four years who did not realize personal integrity and his "word" were his weakest suits. It was not necessarily that he was intrinsically dishonest. If he were, the voters would be able to see it and reject him accordingly.

One idea that made the most sense which was floated around in conservative circles was that the President was an *existentialist*, someone who simply lived from day to day in a world where promises expired at sundown. Clinton could promise the moon to Smith on Tuesday and to Jones on Wednesday and justify the inconsistency in his own mind as a form of *force majeure*. This is the option available only to the paramount leader, permitted to operate outside the rules on behalf of the general good.[1] Throughout most of history, the masses of ordinary people have seemed to accept a double standard for the rules that guide their lives and the rules that guide the life of the leader. At least as long he is moving the ship in the right direction, he is given *some leeway* in his personal characteristics.

Another way to explain Clinton's inconsistencies was a metaphor of a mouse at the entrance to a maze, at the end of which was a piece of cheese. He could sniff the cheese – perhaps simply the goal of re-election – and run up and down the maze, in one direction and then another, because he really had no better idea than his nose on how to get where he wanted to go. The American people accept him with all his flaws and inconsistencies, happy enough to have a President who at least keeps moving in the right general direction by trial and error. Clinton's hero was Franklin Roosevelt, who was in fact the model of the trial-and-error President, re-elected three times by throwing dogma to the winds. By contrast, Ronald Reagan entered the maze with a road map in his head that carried him through with only an occasional wrong turn.

Over the years, Dick Morris had figured out Clinton and also knew they were a good political match. Morris writes this truly excellent summation of the President's political essence:

> Bill Clinton's intelligence is characterized by tremendous strengths punctuated by blind spots. He absorbs and retains data at incredible speeds with pinpoint accuracy and near total recall. He knows endless facts and perfectly encodes the exact advice he gets from each source, down to the slightest nuance. He carries these details in his brain while he works through a decision. But he finds it hard

---

1 Michael Kelly, "The President's Past," *The New York Times Magazine*, July 31, 1994, p. 20. Kelly, one of the finest young political journalists of the era, was the first to catch this angle on Clinton in this profile.

assigning relative importance to the various facts and opinions. He is slow to see patterns and slower still to see them to conclusions. His perfectionism does not permit the rough assumptions from which to build the general theories that are vital to decision making. Of course, once Clinton reaches a decision, he is superb at communicating it to the greatest of intellects and the least educated of people. He reaches them both.[2]

From this perspective, Clinton's management mode of operation is suited to a political executive, as opposed to a political legislator. When he began his first term, he consciously thought of himself in the pattern of Franklin Roosevelt, an executive throughout his luminous career in politics. Unlike Ronald Reagan, who came to the White House with a picture of what he wanted to achieve and how he would do it, FDR arrived with the U.S. economy spiraling out of control and the rest of the world already beginning its steady slide toward Depression and a resumption of the First World War. He didn't have a clue how to fix what he found, but he demonstrated a willingness to try almost anything in order to find something that would work. Ordinary people most appreciated him for his willingness to use the powers of the federal government in new ways, hoping he could find a combination that would bring relief.

In contrast, Clinton was handed a world at peace and an economy already out of the recession President Bush invited with his tax increases. This is not to say he did not face challenges. The *most* serious problem of an economic nature he encountered were public-finance projections of national bankruptcy that would not come to a crisis stage until sometime in the early 21st century, after he was gone. He also had the unprecedented problem of an unscripted New World Order, with the United States alone atop a unipolar world. This was no piece of cake. Yet for a young President whose

---

2 Dick Morris, *Behind the Oval Office* (New York, N.Y.: Random House, 1997), p. 164.

only experience was in governing a small, one-party Southern state, with almost zero experience in foreign affairs, Bill Clinton at least had the luxury of time – a fairly secure peace and prosperity during which he could ride up a learning curve. His experience with Hillary's health care initiative taught him a lot about the ways of Washington, mostly that he had misread the desires of the national electorate. Unlike 1933, ordinary voters now hoped he might find creative ways to have the federal government do less in their lives and the lives of their communities and states. His experience with the 103rd Congress, when the GOP minority would not give him a single vote for his tax-and-spend budget, pushed him further up the learning curve – especially when in November 1994 the voters took the Congress away from him. The mouse had bunked his head in one of the maze's blind alleys, and reversed himself to search for new openings.

Bob Dole was a horse of a different color. For more than three decades he had been near the pinnacle of power in the nation and the world. On the other hand, he did not have even the skimpy experience Clinton had as the chief executive of a small state. Elected to the House of Representatives in 1962 and the Senate in 1968, Dole's only brush with executive skills came in the few years he spent as part-time chairman of the Republican National Committee while still serving as a Senator. His great success as a legislative leader flowed from his skill at being able to add up the needs and wishes of his fellows and find the center of gravity. In that role, there is a need to grasp the essentials of all the issues of public policy facing a great and powerful nation, but never much need to get to the bottom of any single issue. This is why American politicians of this kind have difficulty being nominated by a major party and elected to the presidency.

Members of Congress who have been elected to the White House have always been *issue oriented*, mavericks in their own parties. Lyndon Johnson was Senate Majority Leader, but it was Senator John F. Kennedy, an upstart who got the nomination and the presidency.

After succeeding JFK following his assassination, LBJ was elected in his own right, but no historian will say his four years were successful. Gerald Ford was a House Minority Leader who became President, upon Richard Nixon's resignation, and his two years were so devoid of vision that he held on to the GOP nomination in 1976 by only a few votes, beating California's Governor Reagan, only then to lose to Georgia's Governor Jimmy Carter.[3]

Then came Gingrich, the most famous House member since Kemp, but for all his brainpower, Gingrich was never an idea man, although he pretended to be. Newt Gingrich, like Bob Dole, has devoted his career to legislation, and like Dole has never been terribly interested in getting immersed in single issues. His Contract With America was a grab bag, the product of pollsters. Bored with detail, Gingrich's interest was in rallying troops under banners, with fixed bayonets. In the process, Newt himself went up a steep learning curve as the first GOP House Speaker in 40 years, which political reporters have come to refer as "Pickett's charge," for the amount of Republican blood spilled.

Everything Dole's team has done since Kemp was chosen in San Diego was to play into the hands of the President's chief strategist, Dick Morris, who wants to have "the voters so frightened by Newt Gingrich that they would re-elect President Bill to continue to protect them." In the coming Sunday debate, "to win the White House and the Congress, Dole has to give a clear picture of how he will proceed from day one...putting the horse of economic growth ahead of the cart of downsizing government, instead of the reverse order that Gingrich employed. He has to convey that in a Dole-Kemp administration there will be no government shutdowns, no train wrecks, no threats to default on the national debt...and no

---

3 At one point in his brief presidency, Ford brought Jim Reichley, a writer from *Fortune* magazine, to work at the White House and told reporters that he was specifically hired to provide "vision."

bombing of foreign countries without serious consultation with Congress. A commitment to produce a brand new tax system by 1/1/2000 is the single most important policy pledge I would make. My guess is that Dole will do none of this, but continue to follow the game plan laid out for him by his pollster."[4]

In that first Clinton-Dole debate on Sunday, the sixth of October, Dole didn't follow any game plan. He followed his own instincts, and he had his finest event of the entire campaign as a result. Republicans who believed Clinton would chew him up, and that it would be all over, were thrilled that he not only made it through in one piece, but that he seemed to have found a footing that might turn things around. Dole came across as the dominant figure, the father of the national family: "The President was not enjoying himself at all, and wanted the debate to be over. Four years ago in the presidential debates, it was Bill Clinton, fresh from Arkansas, who seemed by his demeanor and body language to have the world by the tail, the dominant figure. The President back then, George Bush, was the passive figure, almost a disinterested observer, checking his watch, wanting to go home."[5]

Well and good. From that point onward, whatever happened, Dole had rescued himself from his handlers and presented a true and honest picture of himself to the American people. He had not overcome the fears of a unified Republican government, but there was a basis established for making that happen in the weeks remaining.

In the Gore-Kemp debate that took place the following evening, Wednesday October 9. Kemp was on the spot, especially because of GOP expectations that if he was going to rescue a campaign still trailing badly in the polls, he would be have to clean the Veep's clock. To them, this meant that Kemp had to retreat from the deal he

---

4 Jude Wanniski, "Notes on Campaign '96 IV," Polyconomics, Inc., Morristown, N.J., October 4, 1996.

5 Jude Wanniski, "A Family Matter," Polyconomics, Inc., Morristown, N.J., October. 8, 1996.

made with Dole in August, in which it was agreed he would not play the running-mate role of pit bull and savage the Clinton-Gore team.

> There is nothing [Dole] can tell his audience of 80 million Americans about President Clinton that they already do not know. The people who vote for President on November 5 know more about the President than they know about their church pastor or home town mayor. He has been flayed open these last four years, and it is an insult to the intelligence of the American people for Dole to be spending their money on tv spots to tell them stuff they know and have long ago discounted...The plan to have Dole wag his finger and say 'Clinton...liberal, liberal, liberal,' was at least as ridiculous as the 1988 idea of having Michael Dukakis put on an army helmet and drive a tank around in circles.[6]

On the afternoon of the debate, I faxed Kemp a memo warning him against the advice of those who were eager to see him spill some blood. "The Beltway/Bill Kristol/Ed Rollins crowd wants you to take the gloves off and bash Clinton. Gigot's editorial today in *The Wall Street Journal* is part of that nonsense. They are setting you up for the blame on why Clinton wins. You are supposed to throw away your capital that has accumulated over a quarter century for one cheap shot that would set the campaign back. I send along the endorsement today of *The New York Observer*, which can only be attributed to Dole's refusal play the negative game."[7] Fortunately, Kemp, as is his habit, took the high ground.

---

6 Ibid.

7 Jude Wanniski, Memo to Jack Kemp, October 9, 1996. I cited "Bob Dole, the Right Choice for '96! A Vote for Character Over Sleaze," Editorial, *The New York Observer*, October 7, 1996, p. 1. This was the biggest endorsement shock of the campaign as the *Observer* is a cornerstone of NYC's limousine liberal establishment. In a way, the editorial may have hurt the Dole effort because it left him and his team with the impression that integrity would be enough to win. "Where's the outrage?" Dole would exclaim in the closing days, finding no resonance to the *Observer* endorsement among ordinary Americans.

The debate itself was somewhat of a wash.[8] From the clips on the late news, it was easy to see why the instant polls were easily giving the debate to Gore. A Rhodes scholar, Gore was simply a better debater. Kemp might have lost the debate on Oxford debating points, which is how Gore learned technical debating skills, but when asked who had the better ideas for the future, respondents in the polls said he outpointed Gore. These were among the same people who said Gore won the debate. MSNBC viewers who were polled said 32 percent were more likely to vote Republican after having watched Gore-Kemp, 18 percent saying they were more likely to vote the Democratic ticket.

Even if Kemp had indeed cleaned Gore's clock, there were still significant problems with the campaign. Many business and financial leaders agreed that a break in the minority vote could make a ball game out of the campaign. But there remained too much cynicism about Dole's commitment to a high-growth strategy – especially as there had been so little discussion of it outside of Kemp's efforts. The Dole paid media effort remained as dismal and ineffectual as it had been all year. "If Dole is going to produce any surprises in his Wednesday debate with Clinton, it had best involve some kind of an initiative or iron-clad promises that will dissolve the last, remaining doubts about a unified Republican government. The nation's women, who are justifiably concerned about the risks of a Dole-Gingrich assault on spending, are not going to be persuaded by the men of the family that the risks are worth taking unless something

---

8 I did not watch the Gore-Kemp debate. On the afternoon of the debate, I was addressing the Financial Analysts Society of San Francisco. At noon the next day, I was scheduled to speak to the Financial Analysts Society of Los Angeles, so I was on an airplane while Kemp and Gore were waltzing around. All I got live, on the taxi radio in LA on the way to my hotel, were the closing statements of the two men, and on that count there was no doubt that Jack had bested Gore. I told both analysts societies that I would be somewhat surprised if Dole-Kemp did not win. This was an outrageous position to take, but I based the assessment on what I thought Dole would do in the last four weeks, which never came to pass. This is recounted in "Why Dole-Kemp Should Win," Polyconomics, Inc., Morristown, N.J., October 11, 1996.

is put forth to clinch the deal. George Bush did it in 1988 with his 'read my lips' pledge, but the breaking of that pledge is now a large part of Dole's problem."[9]

As time ran out, Dole put all his chips of the "Trust Me" theme. It was his last, best shot, but not unless he told the voters *what* they should trust him to be like as President. In early October, I began suggesting to Kemp that he encourage Dole to make a list of campaign promises – not of *things* he would propose or deliver, but of *how he would behave*, a list of principles that would guide him in the Oval Office. Jack told me there was enthusiasm for the idea and that his staff was mulling over a draft I had prepared. I learned they thought six or so of the ideas were good and that they were brainstorming themselves.

Once the voters had been reminded that Dole is a man of his word and can be trusted, they needed to be told what it is he can be trusted to do. A President can't "promise" to deliver any piece of legislation or constitutional amendment. All he can do is ask Congress, and everyone knows how fruitless an enterprise that can be. "These, though, are his own Secular Ten Commandments. They are things we all know Dole will be able to do, and that he will be *happy* doing so. Yet they all, singly and in combination, present the picture of a good and wise President. The reason you can do this at the last minute – simply releasing it in a press statement and still have it change votes by the ton – is that it will not cost you a penny for advertising. The list of ten will be read on all the radio shows, will scroll down the TV screens of all the network news shows, and will run in a box on the front pages of most American newspapers."[10]

1. **I promise never to shut down the federal government.** This
   is obviously a slap at Newt [Gingrich]. It announces Dole's

---

9 Jude Wanniski, "Why Dole-Kemp Should Win," Polyconomics, Inc., Morristown, N.J., October 11, 1996.

10 Jude Wanniski, Memo to Scott Reed, October 21, 1996. In a rationale to the Dole campaign manager, I attempted to further explain the idea behind these ten promises.

respect for the government and infers its importance as a continuing agent of assistance to the people. It also suggests that he did not approve of what Newt did, which he did not, but does not say so directly. By leaving it at that, it could be taken as a joint apology, on behalf of the whole GOP, for the senselessness of the train wreck Newt engineered.

2. **I promise never to threaten default on the national debt of the government.** This was the single most shocking thing that Newt [Gingrich] said publicly during his face-off with the White House. Until that point – [a] "Meet the Press" interview – the public did not know who was to blame for the showdown. Newt's statement saying he did not care if we defaulted was totally irresponsible, and I knew the instant the words came off his lips that he had committed a mortal sin. To this day he has not apologized for this. For Dole up front to make this pledge is another piece of Gingrich garbage he simply has to clear off the decks. Again, he should properly leave it at this, not disavowing participation with Newt, as he would seem small if there was not an inference that he accepts some of the blame for going along with Newt.

3. **I promise never to interfere in the elections of a foreign country.** I don't remember a President taking sides in a foreign election the way Clinton did in Israel. It is bad enough to do it in wartime, to have the CIA throw a bone to a favorite, but it is a terrible thing to do in peacetime. Clinton obviously sees nothing wrong with the Indonesians influencing our elections or the United States interfering in the elections of others. The single statement above is all that Dole needs to say, and people around the world will breathe a sigh of relief. Their friends here in the U.S., who will vote on November 5, who constitute millions of votes that are most likely to go to Clinton for other reasons, will be sorely tempted to come to Dole on this promise alone. It will have

great resonance in California, where the Asian-American vote absolutely does not want Washington sticking its nose into the delicate maneuvers going on in Tokyo, Manila, Beijing, Taiwan and throughout the region.

4. **I promise never to use military action against a foreign country without consulting the Democratic and Republican leaders of Congress.** This speaks for itself. It is a crusher for Clinton. People who do not know what Dole is talking about will think about it for a second, ask their husband, and then realize Clinton is a bomber. You don't have to add a word. It would be better if Dole did not.

5. **I promise to keep my door open to any foreign heads of state who wish to seek reconciliation with the United States.** Reconciliation is the most basic of all human political instincts. It failed with Cain and Abel. It is the hallmark of all Good Kings and Good Czars. It is represented in the biblical story of the prodigal son. It presents a picture of Bob Dole being willing to open his door to Castro – who will entertain the Pope in Havana next year, and to all the other bad guys in the world. It establishes the United States as a place where all dissidents can hold out hope for reconciliation, which means we could expect an end to terrorism on our shores from foreign vigilantes. People are smart enough to know this and smart enough to know that Dole knows this too.

6. **I promise to keep my door open to the petitions of any American citizen who believes he or she is being treated unjustly by their government, and to those who believe they or their relatives have been unjustly imprisoned.** This is the Good King among his own people. I told Jack that I learned 30 years ago, spending a week with Lester Maddox in Georgia, why he had the image of a racist, yet got most of the black vote. Like Abe Lincoln, he had a people's day, where folks would line up around the block with petitions for sons

or nephews, or relief from an unjust state tax collector, etc. One in ten would get relief. At Thanksgiving each year, he would pardon a few hundred men and women, who would owe their freedom to their parents, not the parole board. It was rare indeed that they went back to crime. You would think the 90% who got no satisfaction might be mad at him, but they knew they would get another shot next time. He was too rare a man to turn out. I asked him why he had the most liberal Democrat in Georgia as his welfare director, and he said "When you are dealing with poor people, you have to have a heart."

7. **I promise to work with the majority and minority in Congress and with the governors of the 50 states in producing a new federal tax system that is fairer, simpler and permits the optimum development of the individual potential of all our citizens.** He cannot promise a tax cut or a new tax system, but he can promise to work with people who can deliver. This promise lets the whole country know that there is not a single system he has in mind that benefits 51% at the expense of 49%. President Dole will let the people's representatives work this out, and when they have reached a consensus, he will sign what they bring to him.

8. **I promise to do everything I can to raise the standard of living in the United States so that once again it only requires one breadwinner to support a family.** This is in the same spirit, but it sets forth a goal that has real meaning, not some GNP number, or "doubling the size of the economy," which can mean four times more for me, nothing for you. It lets people know that Dole has his vision straight.

9. **I promise to do everything I can to encourage a spiritual and cultural renewal in America by using the bully pulpit of the office of the President.** This alerts all the women who are afraid of Dole, thinking he and Newt will strong arm Congress into passing all kinds of harsh social legislation – for which

they are not ready – that you think primarily of the bully pulpit when it comes to drugs, abortion and school prayer.

10. **I promise to practice forgiveness and reconciliation with our political opponents after November 5, in the spirit of President Ford's pardon of President Nixon.** This tells the country you will be fair with Clinton and Hillary, if it seems they will be indicted for political crimes. We all know this is the danger of turning out President Clinton on November 5 and having him spend the next ten years and every cent he has from his pension defending himself against stuff that has been dredged up by GOP opponents. It says Dole will seriously consider pardoning them for whatever, and will seriously consider pardoning the McDougals, etc. You will liberate the country from a sordid, messy situation that will make us all unhappy for a long time. By putting it in the context of Nixon and Ford, Dole signals a symmetry to his own troops, who will reluctantly concede that what is fair is fair.

I did not expect Dole to even consider making these ten promises in person, but thought he might issue them as a press release, timed to make the Sunday talk shows and newspapers. Within the next 24 hours, the campaign had signed off on having Dole make the "promises" the topic of his Saturday radio address on October 26. The initiative appeared to have scored, though there might only be six promises, but the only hint of what had survived was the report that my Lester Maddox promise of an open door was a general favorite. The promise to hint at a pardon for the President and Hillary was a definite no-no, and Promise No. 5 about keeping an open door to foreign heads of state was probably going to be scratched, on the grounds that Dole would almost certainly reject it.

The concept of international reconciliation as part of the next phase of a new world order was an unqualified bellringer. The idea of having President Dole open to international reconciliation with all our leftover foreign adversaries – Castro, Khadafy, Saddam Hussein,

etc. – was of the ten on the list the most important. It was also the
one most uncharacteristic of the public image of him, yet one that
Dole would be comfortable with. If Dole's commander in chief
refused to hear a petition from a foreign adversary, Dole would
publicly back him up. But if Dole were commander in chief, he
would soften.[11] There was in him the kind of spirit of reconciliation
that led his political mentor, Richard Nixon, to make the historic
breakthrough to China. It is much easier to conduct foreign policy
if the chief executive is prepared to seriously consider petitions
addressing the grievances of other nations.

On that last Saturday in October, I tuned in to hear Dole's penul-
timate campaign radio broadcast, wondering how many of the ten
promises would make it. When the broadcast began with Elizabeth
Dole's voice, it was plain there would be no "trust me" promises at
all. Despite all the assurances I'd gotten from Kemp and the campaign staff, at the last minute Dole decided to turn the mike over to
his wife for yet another endorsement of her husband. That was the
end of it. The Zogby poll had tracked Dole to within 5.3 points of
Clinton with 6 days to go, which again demonstrated that the campaign could have been won with almost any creative strategy in
those closing days.

It was all over. John Zogby, who had the most accurate of all the
tracking polls, on Saturday wrapped it up with a conclusion that the
numbers had widened again and it seemed likely Dole could not
win. Instead of doing anything substantive, the last gasp of the campaign would be Dole's marathon finish, to demonstrate his body

---

11 In the fall of 1993, Representative Charlie Rangel, the Harlem congressman,
had asked me to help in an initiative to bring about a reconciliation with Cuba. I
agreed to look into the possibilities and after satisfying myself there was at least a
slim chance of success brought the matter up with Dole. I told him Rangel had
arranged an invitation from Havana for me to meet with Castro's top aides and
maybe Castro himself, but I would not go ahead if he, Dole, would ask me not to
do so. I said I needed at least his passive assent, which he gave me. On the way out
of his office, I asked him if he had any message for Fidel. "Tell him to shave," Dole
wisecracked.

could take the punishment. He had come to believe that he lost the 1988 GOP nomination to George Bush because Bush could be seen vigorously shoveling snow in New Hampshire, while he sat in his hotel room, with his withered right arm, watching on television. It was no substitute for strategy, but this poignant gesture was gallant and left the image of a man going down fighting to the last. He did what was expected of him by the party, which had survived, but not gained any new ground.

The First Race
of the 21st Century

By all accounts, including this one, the 1996 presidential race was oddly inconclusive. On the surface, almost nothing changed. The President was re-elected without a plurality in the popular vote, as he had first been elected in 1992. The Republicans lost a few seats in the House but retained control, and even picked up a few, in the Senate. If the electorate said anything, it was that its government should continue to do what it had been doing the previous two years. To my mind, this is because the electorate had no better choices. People know that much larger issues must be addressed. These include the usual questions that face a nation after a long period of war, in this case the Cold War, having to do with demobilization, reorganization and reform. They also have to do with America's responsibilities as the only superpower on earth. These issues lurked just beneath the surface in 1996. They will be the issues the presidential candidates and their respective political parties almost certainly will face in 2000. In the process, the two parties will accelerate a major political realignment already begun, one that will make the 2000 race among the most interesting and important in the memories of most Americans.

The topic of political realignment is one that has occupied theorists for at least the past 25 years. When I first heard it discussed almost that long ago, it was supposedly right around the corner. There would be shifts in voting patterns leading to a different combination of voters in the two major political parties. Somehow the shifts would involve liberals and conservatives of different types and locations rearranging themselves by different rank and file. In retrospect, it is easy to see the process of *regional* realignment obviously began in 1964, when the Republican presidential nominee, Barry Goldwater, broke the Solid South that had voted automatically for the Democratic nominee since the Civil War. At Goldwater's passing in 1998, most accounts attributed the regional realignment to him, but it almost certainly was the result of John F. Kennedy's decision in the 1960 race to align himself with the interests of southern blacks by supporting Martin Luther King, Jr., while Richard Nixon implicitly sided with the interests of southern whites in what became known as the Republican "Southern Strategy." Thirty-five years later, there is scarcely a place in Dixie that has not voted Republican in one race or another and it is safe to say that regional realignment has been completed. This does not mean Dixie is now *solid* for the GOP, only that from now on neither party has a guaranteed grip on any of the seats in the region.

By my own litmus test, realignment by rank and file will be complete when a significant fraction, at least 25 percent, of black Americans feel comfortable in the Republican Party, the level now reached by Hispanic and other minority blocs. This doesn't mean realignment has to do with race, although that is part of it. In the largest sense, the electorate has to sort itself out into debating teams more appropriate to the times. This idea was first suggested to me in the spring of 1996, in a telephone conversation I had with Felix Rohatyn. A dyed-in-the-wool Democrat, who also happens to admire Ross Perot, he told me he thought the central political problem in the U.S. today is that both major parties represent the bond market but neither represents the stock market. What Rohatyn was saying struck me as being exactly correct. The bond market represents *security* and the stock market represents *risk*. If both major parties identify *security* as their operating paradigm, policies and attitudes that involve *risk* cannot hope to advance. This is why black Americans remain concentrated in the Democratic Party, including a great many who prefer individual Republicans. They will give the

Senate Majority Leader Trent Lott a majority of their votes in Mississippi. And they will even give a Republican like New Jersey's Governor Tom Kean a superplurality of 63 percent as they did in his 1985 re-election. But because they have the smallest cushion to withstand a period of economic distress, they can't *risk* having the government in Republican hands unless they can be sure the GOP will leave in place the social safety net woven by the Democrats.

In identifying the two parties with Democratic security versus Republican risk, we should think not only of bonds over stocks, but also of blue chips on the NYSE over upstarts on the NASDAQ. In addition to thinking of minorities over whites, we should think of older people who require security over younger people who are eager to take risks that can have high rewards. We should think of big, mature corporations and banks over the new kids on the block, of budget balance over economic growth. In foreign affairs, think of the Pentagon over State, isolationist containment over constructive engagement, force over diplomacy. As it is, Democrats and Republicans each have elements of security and risk, *but the dominant force in each party is security*. The Establishment, which is by its very nature a defender of the status quo, controls both parties. It does so through money and political influence, of which older people and enterprises tend to have more compared with those on the way up. The Establishment likes things the way they are, which is why it is so nervous about political realignment. As things stand, money counts as much as it does because of the federal tax system. When even the smallest favors on Capitol Hill or in Treasury regulations can mean millions or even billions at stake, it makes perfect sense for the Big Guys to buy both parties with whatever it takes.

The government always will have favors to grant to those who seek them, but to stamp out the rampant corruption that mires both parties requires reform of the tax system. If it were drastically simplified, power would flow out of Washington. If unable to threaten individual corporations or entire industries with penalties on them or with subsidies to their competitors, the White House and Congress would find the amount of money available for political campaigns drying up overnight. Without this major source of corruption, Congress could more easily be trusted by the people it represents. Yet, because this would be such a drastic change to the *status quo*, the Establishment would fight it out of fear of what would replace it. By controlling both political parties, it can maintain the *status quo* forever. Only a successful third party presidential candidate or a political realignment of the major parties can produce a clear mandate, a willingness to take the risks on behalf of fundamental reform. A third party presidential candidate might provide such a pivot to realignment, but it is more likely it would be a major party candidate who also would win the nomination of Perot's Reform Party.

John Sears has also talked about a primary theme of the next several elections being *what kind of capitalism are we going to have? What mixture of risk and caution?* This is one way to interpret Perot's entrance on the political stage in 1992, as he came from the side of risk, which was not being adequately represented by the two Establishment parties. Perot did not get to be the most successful entrepreneur of his generation by playing it safe. The two major parties and their friends in the Establishment combined to fend him off in 1992, but his Reform Party remains a force to contend with in 2000. Not that he himself will run, but that his party could nominate one of the major party candidates. The GOP is far more likely to crystallize as the more entrepreneurial of the parties, the Democratic party being more identified with security. If Jack Kemp or Steve Forbes had been the Republican nominee in 1996, I'm almost certain they would have gotten the Reform line on the ballot.

The realignment would be most evident in the voting patterns of black Americans, who were decisive factors in the last major realignment of the parties during the years of the New Deal, an alignment that grew out of the Great Depression. Prior to 1932, black Americans voted Republican as a bloc, identifying with the party of Lincoln. The national Democratic Party relied upon the solid white vote of the Old Confederacy, which maintained strict racial segregation. As the Depression forced desperate young blacks out of the South in search of a livelihood, it also broke their remaining nostalgic ties to the GOP as they swarmed into the Democratic Party. The New Deal at least offered the promise of government jobs and a bit of bread on the table from the Democratic political machines of the big cities. Older blacks remained in the Republican Party, horrified that their children would join the party of poll taxes, lynch mobs, and slavery, but as they died out, the Democratic hold on the black community was complete. By 1960, John Kennedy identified himself with Martin Luther King, Jr., at a time when King was still viewed as a dangerous radical by many Americans and an *agent* of change. Richard Nixon chose instead to identify with Jackie Robinson, a *symbol* of change. Since 1964, the national Republican Party essentially has written off the black vote at the national level. Bob Dole and Jack Kemp only gave lip service to black Americans in this race, the campaign staff refusing to commit any funds to a media effort.

Now that the conversion of the old Confederacy to a two-party system is complete – the GOP having taken root alongside the Democratic Party – realignment finally can be realized. The reason I became interested in the Nation of Islam's Minister Louis Farrakhan – at the time of his Million Man March in October 1995 – is that he appeared to be a genuine agent of change in the context of political realignment. More than any other black leader, Farrakhan represents a reaction to the *security* of the New Deal coalition. His conflict with the Jewish Lobby is political, not religious or social, which is why Minister Farrakhan can insist he is not anti-Semitic or bigoted or a purveyor of hate. In the symbiotic relationship of the New Deal coalition, the Jewish community has supplied money and political skill, which it has in abundance, while the black community has supplied votes, which it has in abundance.

Epilogue

If the Republican Party is going to be given a chance of running an undivided government, in control of the executive and legislative branches for the first time since 1953, it will have to present a presidential nominee who can win black and minority votes. This is not a mathematical statement, but one that takes into account the nature of the presidency. The national consensus is troubled by a GOP center of gravity that insists on being "color blind" on race while there are still legitimate issues that cannot be blind to color. As long as the electorate remains troubled on this point, it will opt for divided government. The national electorate has no choice. It has to, in order to prevent the minorities in the United States and *different* people around the world from losing confidence in American leadership. There are a dozen Republican presidential hopefuls who have no concept of why they do not stand a chance of winning, simply because they ultimately are viewed by the electorate as so insensitive on racial issues that there is no hope of them moving toward a solution of this age-old problem.

It is becoming increasingly obvious to the black community that its role in the long-standing Democratic coalition no longer quite makes sense to the black community. Younger blacks are especially open to the argument that in the past 30 years the black community has been ravaged by the generosity of the welfare state — which was basically all the old coalition had to offer in exchange for the black vote. The several million blacks who circumvented or surmounted the welfare trap are especially open to a new political deal. At my client conference in Boca Raton, Florida, in late February of 1997, Minister Farrakhan stood and applauded when Representative John Kasich [R-OH] said, "It is a sin for the government to do for people what they can do for themselves." In his presentation, Farrakhan asked: "What is left for the black husband and father to do in his family when the government provides free food, clothing, and shelter?" It was noteworthy to observe Representative Jesse Jackson, Jr., a Chicago Democrat, in an MSNBC interview with Tim Russert in

April 1997 speak *glowingly* of Minister Farrakhan "knocking on the door of the Republican Party."

Farrakhan's standing with his fellow Americans is a sign of how wide a gap there is between white and black America. By any measure, among blacks he is the most admired of all their leaders, and yet he is anathema to almost all of white America.[1] The fact that he is Islamic and most of black America is Christian is yet another sign of how little black America is understood by whites. *How can they show him so much respect when he is not of the same faith?* In contemplating the first presidential race of the 21st century, we should find ourselves hoping that this contest could be the key to finally bridging this racial divide in our national family. Perhaps it would involve Louis Farrakhan and the Nation of Islam in some way. Maybe it is destined to come in some other way, but it surely will involve a willingness by the white majority to deal with the leader *chosen* by the black minority – not someone *preferred* by whites. In addition, it does seem axiomatic that this coming to terms at home has to occur before the rest of the world feels truly comfortable with permitting the United States to instruct it on proper behavior in human rights.

It is Reverend Jesse Jackson, Sr., who identifies with welfare, security, and all the various government affirmative actions. It makes more sense for younger blacks to be throwing their support behind the growth wing of the GOP, for example, supporting economic policies that encourage economic growth, such as elimination of the

---

1 Minister Farrakhan has, of course, said things critical of the Jewish *political establishment* from time to time, but in reviewing more than a hundred hours of audio and video tapes of his speeches and interviews, I could find nothing I considered mean-spirited, let alone bigoted. I've spent almost as much time with him in person and on the telephone and never once has he let slip a remark or sign that I could consider unworthy of a man of God. He acknowledges flaws in several of his attempts to be understood, but the failure to communicate accurately is almost entirely on the white side, Jewish and Christian. This explains to me why the great majority of black Americans sees him as a *good* man while whites have been persuaded that he is not.

capital gains tax, which has become the defining economic issue between the parties. Without these younger blacks who would benefit most from entrepreneurial capitalism, the GOP's growth wing loses one battle after another to the corporate statists who automatically prefer their own security over new opportunities for potential competitors.

The same division between risk-taking and security occurs in the realm of foreign policy. Just as the major corporate players have "bought" the two major parties to ensure security over risk, and the Cuban emigre community has "bought" both major parties on its issue of opposition to Castro, the Jewish community has used its clout to persuade both major parties to support Israel's stance against the Islamic world, with little or no debate. The Cuban and Jewish lobbies each have a perfect right to do so, but it is not clear their interests or the U.S. national interests are served without a debate that takes up alternative arguments, concerns, and perspectives.

In a realignment of the parties, that would produce a GOP party of entrepreneurial risk, U.S. foreign policy likely would be more open to reconciliation with Cuba as well as a healthier exchange of views with the Islamic nations of the Middle East. The U.S. should receive petitions for reconciliation from all nations, especially the so-called "rogue states" of Iraq, Iran, Libya, and the Sudan. The Jewish political community, which is divided on almost all other issues, is united on Israel's security, unwilling to chance a political realignment that might threaten it. When Jack Kemp had a good word to say about the Million Man March during the 1996 campaign, Jewish political leaders came down on him like a ton of bricks, no matter that his past support for Israel's security had been beyond question. Similarly, General Colin Powell is anathema to all the foreign-policy hawks, not only those in the Jewish and Cuban communities. Kemp and Powell are natural allies, willing to take chances on economic growth and on foreign policy initiatives in a new world order.

Epilogue

The refusal of the Jewish political lobby to deal with the Nation of Islam should soften at the point it is clear it can help bring about a secure peace for Israel *because* it has the confidence of the Arab world and also supports the independent Israeli state. Jeffrey Goldberg, a columnist for the Jewish English-language weekly, *The Forward*, was surprised to find this out in an early 1998 interview with Minister Farrakhan: "I was surprised to hear him express a viewpoint analogous to that of the Israeli Labor Party. 'I think there's a new hope for peace in the Middle East, and I believe that Prime Minister Rabin saw this...What Rabin wanted to pass on to his grandchildren was a legacy of peace. If he felt he could trade land for peace, then he felt that that was a good political step for him to take. I felt that that poor man was on the road that could have led to lasting peace. Those accords would have led to Palestinian sovereignty and an interrelationship with Israel as states relate to each other.' Farrakhan even waxed philosophical about Israel's greatness. 'What was the land like before the Jews got there? It was barren. Now what is it now that you have been there for 40-some odd years with the help of the U.S. and of Jewish people from around the world? You have produced in the desert something magnificent.' Not the sort of language I expected from Louis Farrakhan."[2]

The reason to dwell on Farrakhan and the Nation of Islam is that they practically are a metaphor for the contradictions in American domestic and foreign policy that have to be addressed sooner or later, with the 2000 presidential race an obvious opportunity: white

---

2 Jeffrey Goldberg, "The Farrakhan Effect," *The Forward*, June 19, 1998, p. 7. In the first of two columns devoted to the interview, "Farrakhan the Chasid," which appeared on June 5, Goldberg explained his interest in talking to Farrakhan: "For a man who seems to despise Jews so ardently, he spends a good deal of time worrying about his relations with them." The comment suggests the communication gap between blacks and Jews, when Goldberg could so casually note that Farrakhan "seems to despise Jews so ardently." I can find nothing but admiration for the Jewish people in Farrakhan's taped speeches dating back to 1984.

vs. non-white; rich vs. poor; the powerful vs. the disenfranchised; Christians and Jews vs. Muslims. The world's only superpower is undeniably dominated by white men of European heritage who are Christians and Jews, while Farrakhan embodies all that they are not. Reconciliation is just a matter of time, as the same positive forces that are beginning to bring the Catholic Church and China together have now brought the Vatican close to positive relations with Cuba and Libya. Americans of all stripes eventually will see Farrakhan as a positive force in the Middle East. A perfect example was his break-through in Philadelphia, which was scarcely mentioned in the national press – although *The New York Times* had a very respectful account of it. It was the first time he had been asked by a white politician, Mayor Edward Rendell, a Jewish Democrat, to help solve a problem of racial division. The *Philadelphia Inquirer* reported the following Sunday that Rendell's mail had been running at 50-to-1 in favor of his invitation to Minister Farrakhan, *after* the minister's 85-minute speech the previous Friday. Jewish Philadelphians are divided on whether he did a good thing or not.

As in 1932, a political realignment would not occur overnight. As a result of the Million Man March, 1.7 million more black men voted in 1996 than in 1992. This was a marked change from the results of Jesse Jackson's voter registration drives in 1984 and 1988, which succeeded more with black women than black men. As black men see something they can believe in that is possible in the political realm, after decades of disappointment, their voter participation should continue to increase. The GOP opening can occur not because the GOP offers the black community *things* in exchange for votes, but because of an offer of a share in the political power of party governance. It is hardly a secret that all the black political leaders are rooting for this kind of a scenario. Black political influence can only mature when both parties simultaneously are competing for it. The Jewish vote, which is now almost as solidly Democratic as is the black vote, would also divide, the younger population drifting into the GOP's party of risk. The Hispanic vote has already shifted along these lines. When the top leaders of black and Hispanic organizations are asked what they need most in their communities, the answer is usually the same: access to *capital and credit*.

* * * * *

In electing its President, the electorate does its best to choose the right man for the job at hand, given the choices available. The job seeks the man, not the other way around. In thinking about the first race of the new century, we can examine this proposition as we look back through the last half century to get a sense of what is ahead.

In 1952, the right man at the right time was General Dwight D. Eisenhower, a man skilled in the art of war and peace at a time the nation had become mired in the Korean War. As such, foreign policy took precedence over the domestic economy as Eisenhower won the GOP primary from Senator Robert Taft of Ohio, who had pledged to cut the income tax by a third from its 91 percent top rate. During the campaign, Eisenhower hinted at a tax cut too, but as soon as he was inaugurated, he told a press conference the tax cut the Republican congressional leaders introduced as HR 1, a 30 percent tax cut, would have to await a balanced budget. He also asked for an extension of the excess-profits tax because he said he "needed the revenue."[3] Ike ended the war, but the economy dragged through his eight years. In 1960, John F. Kennedy promised to get the economy moving again and squeaked by Richard Nixon. The Kennedy tax cuts, passed after his assassination in 1963, did bring rapid economic growth, but JFK left another military quagmire as his legacy, in Vietnam.

---

3 *In The Way the World Works*, my 1978 book, I termed this "the worst decision of [Eisenhower's] presidency." I also noted: "Senator Taft, furious, predicted that the Republicans would deserve to lose the 1954 elections if they did not both cut tax rates and balance the budget." In fact, they lost the 1954 elections and did not regain the House for 40 years.

Epilogue

Note in this pattern the inability of recent presidents to simultaneously succeed at home and abroad. President Lyndon Johnson had passed the Kennedy tax cuts, which the Goldwater Republicans had opposed. But he sank the country deeper into the Vietnam War and was finally persuaded to raise taxes to help finance it, a move that weakened the economy and led LBJ, in despair, to take himself out of the running for a second term in 1968. The Republican, Richard Nixon, who was defeated in 1960 when the domestic economy was the issue, was elected on the strength of his promise to end the Vietnam War and to end the Vietnam War tax. Once again, we had a GOP President who succeeded in foreign policy, ending the Vietnam War and developing an historic opening to Communist China, but who failed miserably on domestic economic policy. Nixon allowed his economic advisors to persuade him to leave the Vietnam War tax on for an extra year, to sign a doubling of the capital gains tax, and finally to go off the gold standard and contain the resulting inflation with wage-and-price controls. Until Ronald Reagan came along in 1980, there had not been an American president since Calvin Coolidge who history could judge as having produced both peace and prosperity.

In that sense, everyone is cut out for what they are doing in life, good or bad, depending on the path they've followed from conception onward. As the perfect example, Ronald Reagan was born in a lower middle-class town family with a good-humored father, an Irish Democrat with a weakness for alcohol. Coming of age in the Roaring Twenties, Reagan's personality was shaped in these anything-is-possible years in America, risk-taking years where initiative was rewarded, the sky was the limit, our destiny as the last best hope of mankind fulfilled. From 1929 to 1932, he went to a small college in Illinois and studied economics just as the economy was moving from boom to bust. He was able to get a job as a radio announcer in Iowa, then took a chance on Hollywood when thousands were doing the same. He made it big enough that he entered the 90 percent income-tax bracket, where he experienced firsthand the discouraging effects high rates have on initiative while having almost none on inherited wealth.

Reagan's entry point into "elective politics" was as president of the Screen Actors Guild after World War II. By being drawn into the union, he experienced the reality of communist inroads being made into the culture, a critical time that turned him toward the Republican Party. The turn did not help his movie career, which led to his association with General Electric and more than a decade of criss-crossing the country making inspirational speeches to grass-roots America, refreshing his own roots. He was an anti-communist, but never a scary one who gave the impression, as Barry Goldwater did, that he might nuke the Soviets. Ibn Khaldun, the 14th century Arab philosopher, who Reagan often quoted, would have approved of Reagan's "gentleness," which Khaldun believed was the most essential ingredient of a great leader.

In 1976, Reagan made a run against President Ford, who had been appointed, not elected to the presidency, and was appreciated by the electorate for doing no harm in his $2^1/_2$ years at the helm. Reagan came within a few votes of the GOP nomination, but he made enough mistakes in the early stages to demonstrate he was not ready. There was still something "Goldwaterish" about Reagan in 1976 that might have seen him defeated by the Democratic nominee, Jimmy Carter, if he had won the nomination from Jerry Ford. The next four years were critical in sanding the rough edges from Reagan as he connected with the economic ideas of Jack Kemp.[4]

Instead of the usual zero-sum Republican nostrums, which required a loser for every winner, Kemp had energized the party with his

---

4 In 1976, Reagan went into the New Hampshire primary with a zero-sum plan to cut $90 billion from federal spending and return it all to the American people with tax cuts. He led in the polls until his research director Jeffrey Bell, who had come up with the plan, released a list of the potential spending cuts. When Reagan stumbled badly in trying to defend the specifics, he abandoned the plan and dropped in the polls, narrowly losing the New Hampshire primary, just enough to lose it all.

tax-cutting ideas that paralleled those of the Roaring Twenties. Instead of having to campaign on a platform of spending cuts on the poor to finance tax cuts for the rich, Reagan could campaign on tax cuts, period. And when he finally got the full effects of his tax cuts, he could turn to defeat of the Evil Empire. He did so with a generosity of spirit that even involved a promise to share our "Star Wars" technology with the Soviet Union in order that we could both escape "mutually assured destruction." In looking back on these years, it is difficult to imagine that any other little boy could have grown up to be suitable for the job of work Reagan accomplished. This is my idea of how democracy works, at least our kind of democracy. The people sow the fields, some seed falls on rocky soil, some on sandy soil, some takes root and flourishes. At the right time, one is ready to be chosen.

In 1988, Kemp sought the Republican nomination, but the electorate needed a president in the next four years who would finish the job of ending the Cold War that Reagan had begun with his Gorbachev initiative. His vice president, George Bush, not only was the only one of six serious contenders for the nomination to support the Reagan initiative – the others, including Kemp, insisted the Soviets could not be trusted. Bush was also the only one of the six whose skills had been thoroughly developed in the area of foreign policy. He had been UN Ambassador, head of the liaison office in Beijing, and director of the Central Intelligence Agency. When he completed the assignment of ending the Cold War without firing a shot, President Bush almost openly showed less interest in the new problems facing the electorate. He had finished the roof on the old house and was not up to the work of starting a new one in 1992.

In 1996, the reason the electorate seemed so attracted to General Colin Powell as a prospective President is because it knows a new house has to be built, a New World Order, and Powell seemed the only American leader to appreciate the dimensions and designs of that task. Indeed, when President Bush completed his central assignment of ending the Cold War, he seemed to mentally shift gears toward his retirement years. Powell was the man to whom he turned as the "building contractor" for the New World Order. For a while, it seemed the general would make his wisdom and experience available to the electorate, but it was clear he was not the man for the job when he was so easily driven off by the Republican right. The right-wing coalition openly denounced Powell for being a social liberal, on the grounds that he was pro-choice on abortion. It was obvious to me this was a thin disguise for their dislike of Powell's view of the New World Order. Specifically, as Bush's National Security Advisor, he was the man who had refused to ignore the commitments Bush made to the Islamic nations who joined the Gulf War coalition. He would not use the full force of our military capability to destroy Iraq's Republican Guard and march into Baghdad to find and kill Saddam Hussein.

Those who took this hardline position seem to be saying "*If the United States is to reign supreme as the Global Sovereign,* it must reserve the right to use its military power whenever and wherever it wishes, regardless of what the United Nations or any collection of lesser states think." The term "triumphalism" best describes this body of thinking. It sounds extreme when stated so baldly, but it does represent an assertion of responsibility as well as power and must be taken seriously in debating the role of the "Global Sovereign" in the management of the world. If the presidential race in 2000 is occupied with this question to any degree, as it will have to be, the Republican candidates naturally will be found closer to this position than will the Democrats. It can be seen in the legislative pressures to withhold U.S. payment of outstanding dues to the United Nations unless the UN reform itself toward principles that are more, well, *Republican.* The world as it exists is still too *collectivist* for GOP tastes, not sufficiently *individualist.* If this wing of the GOP could have its way, the world would also be more spiritual, more religious, more Christian, more docile in submitting to American

Epilogue

interests, with fewer weapons capable of threatening their neighbors, not to mention the United States. Because neither China nor the Islamic world seems to be moving in this general direction any time soon, the GOP's center of gravity will be its most *triumphal* in regard to these two peoples, who together comprise more than 40 percent of the world population. This means a tendency to reach for economic and diplomatic sanctions whenever necessary to keep these *different* kinds of people under control.[5]

We should assume the American electorate is not at all triumphalist at its heart, even while it knows the United States must take primary responsibility for managing the world. It is not likely the voters would choose a President in 2000 who would exhibit a tendency to exclude people around the world who are different or who would choose force before diplomacy had been tried. We learn our basic politics in the family unit, where parents take primary responsibility for managing and who learn the need to find the correct mixture of diplomacy and force. The genius of the U.S. two-party system enables the electorate to balance policy by weighting the executive and legislative branches with hawks and doves. It is safe to say a man as hawkish as Senator Jesse Helms, the North Carolina Republican who chairs the Foreign Relations Committee, is not presidential material. A president simply has too much raw power in the realm of foreign affairs, as commander-in-chief, to be "balanced" by members of Congress. *In this rare peacetime era, the primary work required of the next President will be to design a foundation of lasting peace.*

---

5 In *The New York Times* "Week in Review" section of May 24, 1998, David Sanger notes how difficult the American foreign policy establishment is finding the exercise of economic superpower: "Almost simultaneously, the White House backed down from threats of sanctions against European firms for doing business with Iran and Libya. Those threats sounded tough: Any global company doing deals there was put on notice that it would suffer sanctions in America. The strategy backfired. Rather than create an alliance against terrorist states, it created an alliance against the American assumption that Washington can set foreign policy for the world."

If this assumption is correct, it is more likely the electorate would choose a Democrat such as Vice President Al Gore in 2000 over the queue of Republican hawks who are lining up for a shot at the presidential nomination. The electorate will insist upon a peacemaker in the White House, not an old Cold Warrior itching for a new fight. It will also insist on a President who will keep a Republican Congress from getting ahead of itself in its desire to dismantle federal programs associated with the New Deal and Great Society. Gore is, of course, the heavy favorite to win the Democratic nomination, and, as such, he also should be expected to win the presidency. The chances of him bringing in a Democratic Congress seem almost nil at this point, as the electorate does want progress made in downsizing the federal Leviathan and at the very least will require a Republican Congress to keep a President Gore from turning the government over to the environmentalists. The only possibilities among the Republicans who might win the nomination and the presidency with a GOP Congress are those few who are not identified as foreign policy hawks or cultural conservatives.

Colin Powell is, of course, high on this short list, but his repeated insistence that he will not be a candidate for elective office must be seen as definitive. Texas Governor George W. Bush is being cited as the early choice of the same Republican Establishment that fell in behind the Dole candidacy. By staying aloof from the issues that divide Republicans in Washington, the son of the former President can still be seen a unifier and his popularity in Texas after one term in the statehouse is beyond question. At some point, though, he would have to define himself on the issues that the electorate wishes resolved, and it is not clear that the younger Bush has given much thought to them in Austin, or that he has the advisors who would put him on a constructive path. He is the early favorite to win the nomination in the early public opinion polls, which more expresses a hopefulness about the former President's son more than any knowledge about his ability or readiness for the job. Jack Kemp

Epilogue

already is being counted out by both the Establishment, which always prefers a safe candidate, and by the cultural conservatives and foreign policy hawks, who prefer militancy over peacemaking. Steve Forbes has made his peace with this coalition and so has Senator John Ashcroft of Missouri, but in doing so they are testing the limits of their acceptability to the broad electorate.

The clash between economic and social conservatives in the Republican Party is not at all about social goals and objectives, but about the policy paths by which we get there. The cultural conservatives want strong families, low divorce rates, low crime rates, excellence in education, and a culture as free as possible of abortion, drugs, pornography, homosexuality, and violence. In turning to the government for solutions, they seek the kind of direct action that turns into conservative social engineering, the flip side of the social engineering favored by cultural liberals.

Economic conservatives, on the other hand, tend to believe that governments cannot force people to behave if government tax, monetary, and regulatory policies are causing the economic contraction of opportunities and living standards. Everyone knows the gap between the best and the worst educated has been growing steadily in recent years. Cultural conservatives want the government to divert resources from public schools to private schools to fix the problem, assuming public education to be the problem. Economic conservatives know the children of lower- and middle-income families are not getting the attention at home they should because both parents must work to make ends meet. These families can only afford public schools and expect the schools to educate children who have not been prepared in their homes. Meanwhile, liberals want more federal resources for child care. The objective must be a reconstitution of the one-breadwinner nuclear family and the only way to make that possible is with supply-side growth economics.

The conflict between economic and cultural conservatives surfaced in 1995 when the GOP gained control of Congress and cultural conservatives insisted on legislation to give a $500 tax credit for each child in a family under a specified income level. Their objective was to "strengthen" the family by giving it more money. Economic conservatives instead argued for a capital gains tax cut, to raise capital/labor ratios so real wages would rise for working men and women. This would enable more households to be sustained with one breadwinner. As a result of the conflict, neither tax cut was made in the 104th Congress.

Jack Kemp is the perfect fit, the one GOP candidate who the electorate could trust to put diplomacy ahead of force and racial reconciliation ahead of cultural conservatism. He would have to make the run for the nomination with faith that the Republican primary voters will make that collective judgement. Partly for that lack of faith – a sense he would be rejected by primary voters as he was in 1988 – he decided not to make the race in 1996. By being pulled into the last race of the 20th century to go along for the ride as Dole's running mate, Kemp has acquired a perspective and a confidence that would not have been possible without the experience. And perhaps more faith in the way the voters go about choosing their President. John Sears was probably right that nothing was going to be able to persuade the electorate to choose Dole over Clinton, although Kemp always felt it was within reach – if only ...

My educated guess is that Kemp will win the nomination and the White House because he is the right man for the job at the right time. As Franklin Roosevelt was in 1932, Kemp would be the agent of realignment in 2000. If he does get the GOP nomination, he almost certainly will also get the nomination of Perot's Reform Party. This would provide the pivot for the realignment. This is because people who have been voting Democratic all their lives and refuse to cast a vote for anyone on the GOP line – which includes most black Americans and a great many older blue-collar workers – would be able to signal their preference for Kemp as a reformer, not as a Republican. There is really no other realistic candidate who could be this kind of pivotal figure. It would be a stretch to imagine Texas Governor George W. Bush in this role; his instinct is always corporate, not entrepreneurial, which is why he is the favorite of the Republican Establishment.

Realignment does not simply mean that a lot of people who now vote Democratic will vote Republican. It also means that people who now vote Republican will shift into the Democratic Party, on the margin less interested in risk and more in security. The objective would be two major parties that would provide full-fledged national agendas, each prepared to represent all the people, neither writing off a class nor a community. One simply would tilt more toward security, the other more toward risk. The model is a happy family, in which one parent *tends* toward risk-taking and the other parent *tends* toward security. Each at least is able to appreciate the viewpoint of the other and take it into account in the process of designing family policy. Civility and harmony would replace jealous tantrums and gridlock. As it is, with both parties tending toward security, we get plenty of security and an aversion to risk. The electorate has no choice but to divide responsibility between the executive and legislative branches. After realignment, both political parties would strengthen as entities, one winning a unified government through a cycle of eight or twelve years, the other then designing a platform that corrects in the other direction and winning long enough to carry through.

The happy family should be the metaphor for the next century, not only the family unit but also the family of nations. Because the United States is the only superpower – the global sovereign – for the first time in all of history there is a real opportunity to replace *Realpolitik* with reconciliation in global politics. Within the metaphor of the family unit, *Realpolitik* exists when mother and father are not in harmony. The division leads to a cleaving of the broader family, as they attempt to win over as allies their own children, their friends and their in-laws. At the national or global level, *Realpolitik* was what the Cold War was all about. The United States and the Soviet Union were the competing imperial parents, lining up allies on one side or the other even if it meant pitting otherwise friendly countries against each other. If this meant U.S. coalition with and support for an anti-Soviet authoritarian regime, so it had to be.

With the defeat of the Soviet imperium, the United States must be mother and father to the world. Unless we wish to goad China or the Islamic world into a new Cold War, the concept of *Realpolitik* is now obsolete and so are its practitioners. Picture the countries of the world as children of America as a starting point in thinking of how to manage the global family and it is obvious there is no need for U.S. foreign policy to be built around coalitions and alliances. It also means that, like good parents, the United States not insist that all the children be like the parents in every way. There must be basic principles observed, with the parents setting the example by observing the principles themselves. It will not work harmoniously if the global sovereign insists that every culture and political system be identical to ours. The future of civilization demands that there be continued diversity so that trial and error can continue to produce a dynamic from which everyone can benefit.

We could see this working in the summer of 1998, when President Clinton went to China and gave it a pat on the back for behaving itself as well as it has in recent years. The Republican leadership in Congress and among its intellectuals gave grudging praise for the way the President handled himself, but complained that he had tilted toward Beijing against Taiwan on the issue of Taiwan's status. Of all the Republican presidential possibilities for 2000, Kemp was the only one who offered his support to the President *before* he went to China. But Kemp also joined the other Republicans in making it clear he would not abandon Taiwan's interests. The net effect was a perfect equilibrium, with the United States *as a whole* encouraging the two parties to continue knitting themselves together in myriad little ways. To favor one side over the other would only produce conflict. To give any indication we would support independence for Taiwan would cause its leaders to suspend all efforts at reconciliation. But to allow Beijing to feel we were abandoning Taiwan would also cause its leaders to be less receptive to reconciliation on mutually agreeable terms. The global sovereign was precisely right in its parenting. In this way, we might say the first presidential race of the 21st century had begun, promising elements of realignment, reconciliation and reform that would make it among the most fascinating in American history.

Index

Index

Index

Tax increase of 1993, 43, 61, 85
Vietnam war tax, *v, vi*, 131, 175, 176
Taylor, John, 61, 62, 65, 78
Thatcher, Margaret, 29
"This Week with David Brinkley", 16
Thomas, Clarence, 94
Thompson, Tommy, 145
Thurmond, Strom, 92
Time, 38, 108, 113
Tollerson, Ernest, 57
Tomlinson, Ken, 23, 36
"Train Wreck," See Government shutdown
Tucker, Jim Guy, 82
Twain, Mark, 89

U

United Nations (UN), 105, 120-122, 178-179
USA Today, 97
U.S. News & World Report, 110

V

Van Dyk, Ted, 82
Vanity Fair, 108
Verney, Russell, *ii,* 52-54, 56, 57
Vietnam, Socialist Republic of, 12, 175
Vietnam War, *v,* 176

W

Wallace, Mike, 109
Washington, George, 31, 34

The Wall Street Journal, vi-viii, 11, 12, 16, 17, 20, 53, 56, 81-83, 127, 134, 135, 143, 144, 146, 155
War Powers Act, 118, 123, 128, 129
The Washington Post, 57, 83, 103, 127, 128
The Washington Times, 62
Watergate, 83
The Way the World Works, vii
Weber, Vin, 53, 59, 73, 75-78
The Weekly Standard, 103
Welfare, 16, 55
Welfare Reform, 42, 56
Whatever It Takes, 54
White, Theodore H., *iii*
Whitewater, 81, 82
Whitman, Christie, 28, 31
Wilkie, Wendell, 28, 38
Will, George F., 128
Williams, Armstrong, 25, 33, 94
Wilson, Pete, 94, 145
Witt, Louise, 22, 25
Wolfowitz, Paul, 129
World Bank, 115
World Jewish Congress, 109
World War I, *i,* 151
World War II, *ii,* 113, 114, 177
Wren, Carter, 36-39

Z

Zogby, John, 162
Zuckerman, Mortimer, 110

ABOUT THE AUTHOR

*J**ude Wanniski*** is president of Polyconomics, Inc., in Morristown, N.J., and is one of the leading political economists in the United States. As Associate Editor of *The Wall Street Journal* from 1972 to 1978, he repopularized the classical theories of supply-side economics. His first book, *The Way the World Works,* first published in 1978 to critical acclaim, is now a classic. In it, he forecast both the end of the Cold War and transformation of both the USSR and China into capitalist countries. The passion and eloquence he brought to the supply-side model of political economy became a foundation for the global economic transformation launched by President Ronald Reagan. Wanniski assisted in the design of the historic Kemp-Roth tax rate reforms, helped write the monetary plank of the 1980 GOP platform and served as an unofficial advisor to the Reagan and Bush administrations. He has maintained an active advisory role with various members of the House and Senate of both political parties on the direction of the domestic political economy. He has been an intimate advisor to Jack Kemp for more than twenty years. Throughout his career, Jude Wanniski has focused singularly on the global economic debate on the need for monetary policies that maintain a reliable and predictable unit of account.

Jude Wanniski founded Polyconomics in 1978 to interpret the impact of political events on financial markets. The firm now counsels 200 corporate and financial clients the world over that represent portfolios approaching a trillion dollars. Wanniski and Polyconomics have achieved worldwide recognition for the efficacy of the unique supply-side political-economic model utilized in their analysis. Many of the economic reforms proposed in the firm's classical study, *Mexico 2000,* were implemented by that country's government prior to and during its rapid economic growth of the late 1980s and early 1990s. A division of the company, Global 2000 International Research, provides additional in-depth analysis of world markets. Another division is exploring the Y2K problem, and its potential repercussions and opportunities.

Mr. Wanniski appears frequently in the print and broadcast media, and is a much sought-after speaker for presentations at corporate, financial and political events. Trained in political science and communication, he brings a singular meld of experience in journalism, academia, politics, and business, and demonstrates an uncommon facility in concisely imparting profound information about the unfolding global economy and its expansion into the next millennium. His commentary and daily "Memo on the Margin" may be viewed at <*www.polyconomics.com*>, where he also conducts weekly sessions for students of Supply-side University. He lives in New Jersey with his wife, mother, and two excessively large dogs.